CW01660956

Raymond Foxall w
educated at Urmston Grammar School and Manchester College of Commerce. He entered journalism and after war service joined the *Daily Mirror*, later working for the Press Association and the *Sunday Express*, then joined the *Daily Telegraph*. He has written many books, including several historical novels, and now lives in Perthshire.

Against All Odds

RAYMOND FOXALL

SPHERE BOOKS LIMITED
30-32 Gray's Inn Road, London WC1X 8JL

First published in Great Britain under the title
The Amateur Commandos by Robert Hale Ltd 1980
Copyright © T. Leslie Cuthbertson and Raymond Foxall 1980
Published by Sphere Books Ltd under the title
Against All Odds 1982

TRADE
MARK

This book is sold subject to the condition that it shall not, by way of trade or otherwise, be lent, re-sold, hired out or otherwise circulated without the publisher's prior consent in any form of binding or cover other than that in which it is published and without a similar condition including this condition being imposed on the subsequent purchaser

Set in Lasercomp Times

Printed and bound in Great Britain by
©ollins, Glasgow

CONTENTS

	Foreword	vii
1	Disillusioned Soldier	1
2	An Idea is Born	7
3	The Plot Thickens	14
4	Preparations for Invasion	21
5	Alerting the PM!	27
6	Nearly Caught Out	35
7	The Birds Have Flown	43
8	On the Run	48
9	Waiting for H-hour	54
10	Strange Letter for No 10	61
11	Point of No Return	70
12	Puzzle for the War Office	75
13	The Enemy has Landed	78
14	On the Move	87
15	Sabotage – and Flight	93
16	Back to Sea	100
17	Set for Home	111
18	Ordeal	119
19	Where Are They?	125
20	Suicide Pact	129
21	Court Martial	136
22	Question in the House	145
	Author's Note	151

FOREWORD

This is the true story of a very unofficial operation which took place during the Second World War, conducted by two ordinary British soldiers who were members of a non-combatant unit, a sergeant and a private, entirely on their own initiative and completely without permission from any Army authority.

Amateurs as to fighting techniques and strategy, entirely untrained in any assault methods, they carried out, in secret and on their own, with no assistance from any military source, an operation of the wildest and most quixotic character in a remarkably professional manner, much to the embarrassment but eventual admiration of the military authorities.

The release for public perusal of papers relating to the war years, after being withheld for the requisite period of time, has brought forward many fascinating war stories – none more remarkable than this.

Balgowan,
Perthshire. R.F.

1 — Disillusioned Soldier

When Thomas Leslie Cuthbertson enlisted in the Army on 11th December 1941, at the age of nineteen, when the Second World War had been in progress for more than two years, he could not feel that he had gone to war. Later he was to take part in one of the most unusual wartime incidents ever to occur, an almost incredible two-months adventure, with enough excitement, danger and hardship to last him a lifetime. But not then, not when he was sent for his initial training – posted to a non-combatant unit.

No young man entered the Army with more enthusiasm than he. Impressed by stories of the Great War of 1914-18, told by his father and uncles who had served in it, from childhood he had been fascinated with military matters, and from the outbreak of hostilities he had waited eagerly for his time to join the Army.

From the age of ten he had been an enthusiastic member of the Church Lads' Brigade company attached to his local church at Newcastle-upon-Tyne, preferring the drilling, discipline, army-style ranks and regimental-type bands of the brigade to the Boy Scout movement. The arm of his tunic was smothered with badges he had gained, and attained the rank of staff-sergeant, became his company's physical training instructor, and instead of leaving the brigade at seventeen, continued as an NCO to run the company when all its officers had joined the Armed Forces.

So on the day he attended his interview and medical examination with other young men of an Army intake, and was issued with a uniform, he was excited at the prospect of his forthcoming service, confident that he would be a good if not heroic soldier and that high adventure awaited him.

Six feet and one inch tall, brown-haired, blue-eyed, fresh-complexioned and of erect bearing, he proved, on examination, to be also health category 'A1', a robustly healthy young man.

'Civilian occupation?' It was a question that was to shatter his military aspirations.

'I'm in training as a dental mechanic,' he replied.

'Dental mechanic,' repeated the interviewer, and there was a note of interested surprise. 'We don't get many dental mechanics entering the Army.'

It did not take the recruiting officers long to make up their minds about Private Cuthbertson.

'You will be posted to the Army Dental Corps, Aldershot, where you will be extremely useful continuing your work as a dental mechanic,' he was told.

'I should have liked to go to the infantry.' It was a despairing attempt to realise an ambition – to become what he termed 'a *real* soldier'.

'You will be posted to the Army Dental Corps.' The order was repeated, and it was final.

Private Cuthbertson went to Aldershot and reported to a corps in which he very definitely did not wish to serve. And there, so it seemed then, he would remain for the duration, working in a dental laboratory, wearing a white coat, and as far as he was concerned, not a soldier at all, while the greatest war in history was being waged.

At the barracks at Aldershot he was first placed with other recruits under the charge of an Army Dental Corps sergeant for six weeks' training in drill, marching and some knowledge of the use of arms. The military aspect of this 'square-bashing' was, of course, to his liking, and to him, unlike some of the recruits, it contained no element of drudgery.

The instructor was Peter King, a tough Regular Army sergeant, smaller but older than Cuthbertson, with a fierce moustache waxed to points at the ends, a strutting and apparently stony-hearted disciplinarian of indeterminate age, whose records showed him as being only five years older than Cuthbertson but who must have been at least thirty years of age. To the reluctant recruit to the Dental Corps, Sergeant King was every inch a soldier, a man whom he admired from the first bellowing order to which the squad was treated.

Sergeant King's job was to take charge of the initial drill

course for all recruits to the Corps, including dental surgeons entering as commissioned officers. He at least would never have to work in a dental laboratory.

According to his papers, King had been born in New Zealand and had enlisted in the British Army Dental Corps as a clerk-orderly on 13 March 1939, before the war began, on a normal regular engagement to serve seven years with the Colours and five in the Reserve. Not only was he obviously much older than his stated age: a note had been written into his Army papers that, 'Although he had not declared any previous service, his exceptional qualities as a drill-instructor suggested that he had had some previous military or police service.' There was some little mystery about Sergeant King. He was never much given, as Cuthbertson was to discover, to talking about his previous life, background or family. But that did not concern the Army. He was a good soldier, his conduct was 'exemplary', and it was obvious that his intelligence was high and that he had benefited from a good education.

As befitted a drill sergeant, King was relentless in voice and word, and he was respected if not feared by the raw recruits. It was not long, however, before he found that one of his pupils in his new squad was outstandingly drill-conscious and that his movements on the square were soon immaculate. To this enthusiastic recruit from Newcastle-upon-Tyne he bent a little from the dignity he preserved as a sergeant. Whenever he dismissed the squad after a drill session, he had a few words with Cuthbertson before strutting off to the sergeants' mess.

'You're doing fine, Cuthbertson.'

'Thanks, Sergeant.'

A few days later: 'Had experience of drilling before, Cuthbertson?'

'Only in the Church Lads' Brigade, Sergeant.'

'Better than no previous experience.' The recruit was treated to one of the sergeant's rare smiles.

'I was a staff-sergeant,' said Cuthbertson, proudly. 'Drill-Instructor actually.'

'Excellent, Cuthbertson. Well, let's hope you don't remain a private for long.'

Some time later, towards the end of January 1942, when the six-week training period was nearing completion: 'Guess you're a lad who *wanted* to join the Army, Cuthbertson.'

'I did. Very much. But not this mob,' said Cuthbertson wryly.

'Why not, lad?'

'Because I want to have a go at the Jerries. That's what being a soldier is all about, isn't it? But here in the Dental Corps I'll be stuck making false teeth. Ugh! What a war service that'll be. Not one to be proud of.'

'I can understand your feelings,' said the sergeant. 'But how did you come to get into the Dental Corps, feeling like you do?'

'At the interview before I came into the Army, they asked me what my civilian occupation was. I said I was training as a dental mechanic, and they pushed me into this lot to do the same job I did in civvy street. Wish I'd told 'em a lie now about my occupation.'

King smiled. 'Quite uncharacteristic of the Army actually. "Anyone here can play the piano?" they ask, and when a chap says, "Me, sarge", they usually say, "Well, get that piano shifted from here." I knew a chap who had his flying licence before he was called up. He was dead keen on going into the RAF and training as a pilot. But would they let him? Not on your life. They put him in the Army, in Signals actually.'

As the weeks passed, the sergeant became more and more interested in the young Geordie who was so dispirited with the prospect of soldiering in a dental laboratory. He had good reason for this. As far as King was concerned, Cuthbertson was not the only disillusioned member of the Dental Corps.

'I don't want to be stuck here for the duration either,' he admitted one day to Cuthbertson.

'It's not so bad for you, Sergeant,' replied the private. 'At least you're doing military work as a drill instructor. *You* won't have to work as a dental mechanic.'

'No, I won't. But the way things are going, I'll be stuck here just the same.' King was looking morose.

Cuthbertson had often seen King demonstrating his love of discipline – and in an altogether tough manner, but the private risked the sergeant's displeasure. 'Am I allowed to ask – I mean, why did you join the Dental Corps then?'

'I joined it during peacetime,' King snapped. 'It wasn't bad then. But now there's a war on – and that makes it different. I'd like to see some action.' His voice became less harsh then, and he went on: 'That's why I sympathise with you. To be honest, I feel that my talents, such as they are, could be of greater use to the Army and to Britain if I took part in a real military campaign. I'm not only a drill sergeant, I'm an arms instructor too. I know quite a bit about weapons and don't think I'm boasting if I say I'm not a bad shot either.

'There's another thing too. I'm not married, and I have no close relatives. It wouldn't matter a damn to anybody except me if I got killed. But that's enough about me. What makes you so ambitious to get out of the Dental Corps?'

Cuthbertson thought carefully before replying. 'Don't know really. Don't suppose I'll advance much in the Army, in rank or anything else, so long as I stay working in that dental lab.'

'Do you want to make a career of the Army then?'

'I don't want to stay in the Army for life, but while the war lasts, I want to get on – as far as I can, anyhow.'

'What makes you ambitious then? What's your background? I mean what was your life like in civvy street?'

'I've always wanted to get on. Civvy street? I didn't have a marvellous life.' Cuthbertson began to tell the sergeant about his pre-Army life . . .

He had been born on 5 August 1922, the son of a miner in a coalmining community in the north-east of England, at Mary Street, Gateshead-on-Tyne, and in the early 1920s conditions for colliery workers were far from luxurious. His father was not always in employment, and when he was, his pay was not princely. Cuthbertson spoke of early memories of living with his parents and sister in two rooms in a tenement building. Later they moved to a small house, 226 Helmsley Road, Newcastle-upon-Tyne, the home from which he had enlisted.

'I want something better than that sort of life, a lot better, and I'm damned well going to see I get it. My parents want me to as well. They didn't want me to be a miner, and that's why they put me to training as a dental mechanic. But I want a lot better than that too.'

Cuthbertson did not say much more than that to the NCO, even though they were becoming rather friendly for a sergeant and a private, but it was enough for the older man to deduce quite easily that here was an enterprising and ambitious young man whose instinct to make progress had been born out of the circumstances of his early life.

No. 10511436 Private Leslie Cuthbertson, a member of a devout, church-going family, former choirboy, one-time NCO in the Church Lads' Brigade, though completely disillusioned with the Dental Corps and straining at the leash to go into combat with the enemy, was then quite unaware that he was to take part in a desperate, quixotic and bizarre military adventure that even to the military authorities was outrageous and unbelievable. But the conversations he was having with No. 7536394 Sergeant Peter King were slowly and surely laying the ground-work for it.

2 — An Idea Is Born

January came to an end with a whisper of forthcoming spring momentarily half-hidden in the air. Now and again the wind that blew across the barrack square was not quite so keen, and there were evenings when some off-duty soldiers left off their greatcoats as they went for a pint of beer – but donned them again the next night when winter restored its severity.

The hint of spring loitering on winter's back door unsettled Cuthbertson even more – and he made up his mind to make a move towards the action he now craved.

His frustration had grown into a festering sore in his mind, exacerbated by the conversations he was having with his sergeant. They talked about the progress of the war – if what was happening could be termed progress! It was two years, they recalled, since the German tanks had rolled into France and the Nazis occupied that country. The successful evacuation of the British Expeditionary Force from Dunkirk had been a miracle, but only the English Channel separated the Nazis from England. For a long time, invasion of Britain was a possibility, never very far from the thoughts of British people.

In the Middle East, they knew, the British Eighth Army was squaring up to the German General Rommel, but many British troops were confined to Britain. Cuthbertson and King were not the only soldiers to feel frustrated to a greater or lesser degree, but none were more so than the Dental Corps private and sergeant, neither of whom possessed the British characteristic of phlegmatism.

'The RAF chaps are jolly lucky,' King remarked to him about that time. 'At least they have the satisfaction of striking at Germany with bombs. But what can we do in the Army just now, even if we were in a combat unit?'

'There'd be a chance of having a go in the future,' grumbled Cuthbertson. 'At least we'd be training for the day when we could do *something*.'

It was not surprising the two were disillusioned. Throughout the country there was a deep desire to be getting on with the war, though at that time the position was necessarily static. What *was* surprising was the military operation a sergeant and a private were to dream up . . .

Cuthbertson made his move. 'Will you arrange for me to see the CO so I can ask for a transfer to the infantry?' he asked King.

'That won't do any good,' said King. 'He'll not agree to your request.' He was very confident.

'Well, I want to try it on.'

'I tell you, it's no use.'

'Why not?' Cuthbertson refused to share the sergeant's pessimism. 'Why do you say that?'

'Listen, lad, I'll tell you something now,' said King. 'I didn't tell you before because I didn't want to make you more browned off than you already are. Since this bloody war began, I've asked the CO *three times* for a transfer to a combat unit. Each time he turned my request down – flat.'

The statement silenced Cuthbertson for all of two minutes while he brooded over it. 'Why?' he asked then. 'Why wouldn't he let you go? If you want to fight, why won't they let you? We'll never win the bloody war that way.'

'He won't agree to a transfer – and that's that. It would be nothing but a damned waste of time if I set up an interview for you.'

'Well, I'd still like you to,' urged Cuthbertson, 'and what's more, I'll keep on pestering until I get to see the CO. He might let *me* go.'

'Not a chance. I can tell you exactly what he'll tell you. He'll say the Army has to work as one machine and not for the individual wishes of the men in it, that chaps just couldn't have what they wanted once they were enlisted. He might say that everyone has to do what he's told and that that's what discipline is all about.

'Then he'll tell you that the job of every single soldier is important, and that the men in the front line have to be backed up by thousands who are not – by the supply and medical services, by drill-instructors, as in my case – and by blokes in the dental service like you.'

'Sounds crazy to me,' said the private gloomily. 'As I say, if a man wants to fight, why won't they let him? If a man wants to fight, surely he'll make the best soldier. Anyone can be a dental mechanic.'

'But they can't, you know. How long would it take for them to train a man as a dental mechanic from scratch?'

'I really want you to get me before the CO,' Cuthbertson was adamant.

Early in February Sergeant King arranged the interview, marched Cuthbertson into the CO's room and stood behind him.

'Yes, Cuthbertson?' The officer looked up from his desk. 'What do you wish to ask me?'

'I'd like to apply for a posting to a fighting unit, sir.'

'Are you not happy with us, Cuthbertson?'

The private was momentarily nonplussed. 'It's not that, sir,' he said. 'It's just that I want to be a fighting soldier. That's what I thought I was joining the Army for.' He ran out of words.

'We all find the Army different from what we expected.'

There was a silence, and the sergeant's voice came from behind Cuthbertson: 'Permission to speak, sir. For your information, sir, Private Cuthbertson is my best recruit of the recent intake. He's good at drill, has taken a great interest in arms instruction and is greatly interested in military matters. I'm personally aware, sir, that he is extremely keen to take part in combatant duties.'

'Thank you for your report, Sergeant,' said the officer.

Cuthbertson was more than grateful for it.

'Well, Cuthbertson, we'll have to talk about it.' The officer's voice was cheerful, friendly even, but he was not prepared to see Cuthbertson's problem as more important than that of the Army as a whole. 'We try to do the best we can for the war effort. Don't for heaven's sake think you are not doing important work for the Army. You are. Very important. The work you did in civilian life is of the greatest value to us. The health of the soldiers is a prime consideration, and we in the Dental Corps are helping to keep the Army fit and well. Apart from anything else, I don't want to lose you. There aren't so many men in the Army with your special pre-war training that we can allow one to slip through our fingers. Do you understand that, Cuthbertson?'

'Yes, sir,' said Cuthbertson, understanding the CO's reasoning but privately not agreeing that it should apply to him. 'It's just that I feel that I would be of more use to my country in *another* job. I'm prepared to do anything and go anywhere, sir. Isn't there something more – er, exciting that I could volunteer for? I've heard some special units have been formed – and that you can volunteer to serve in them.'

'I believe there are – and you may be right. But we can't have everybody doing that, now can we, Cuthbertson? After all, you've only been with us a few weeks. Hardly time for you to bed down, eh? Your work is highly valued in this unit. I'd like you to know that. Your wish to serve in a combatant unit is certainly praiseworthy, but there's little doubt that the best way for you to serve, at the moment, is as a dental mechanic. I really don't think there is any possibility of posting you to another unit.'

There was another silence, the officer smiling, the private standing glumly to attention.

'Is there anything else you'd like to say to me?' asked the CO.

The nineteen-year-old had run out of arguments. He also knew that he had lost the verbal battle. 'No, sir,' he said.

'Very well, Cuthbertson. I suggest that you return to your duties, which I'm sure you will find very satisfying. Many men in the Army, of all ranks, are not blissfully happy. I think you'll find as time goes by that you're as happy as most.'

As he marched out of the room, the young hopeful could not agree with the statements that had been presented to him, certainly not the last one.

The CO felt there was reasonable hope that Cuthbertson would settle down to his uninspiring wartime duties. He was to discover, in quite a dramatic manner, that this was not so.

Cuthbertson's desire for military excitement did not abate. He grew more and more unhappy.

There were men in the corps who were reasonably contented. Others, if they had made a bid for a transfer and failed, would have considered they had salved their conscience and settled down. But not Cuthbertson. He became increasingly moody, like an ambitious man who sees others promoted when he thinks it is he who deserves advancement.

In the evenings he changed his laboratory overall for battledress uniform for his off-duty hours. His web-belt and ankle-guards were blancoed to perfection; his boots were polished into black mirrors; no smarter soldier went for a stroll or sat in the canteen, nor was there in the barracks a more erect and soldierly figure.

Sharing a yearning for action, a *cause célèbre* almost, sergeant and private met more frequently, usually in the NCO's private room at the barracks, to discuss their common cause. The gap between their ranks did not prevent a friendship springing up. 'Sergeant' and 'Cuthbertson' became 'Peter' and 'Leslie'. Never for a moment did King relax his discipline while on duty.

They kept up-to-date with news of what was happening in the Forces, some that was published and some that reached them only on 'the grapevine'. They knew that the Prime Minister, Mr Winston Churchill, had ordered that two élite forces be formed and trained, one for seaborne raids when the time came and another to go to war by air. Both had been given the name 'commandos', and the latter were also known as 'paratroopers'. Some of these special-service units had been sent to Egypt to assist General Wavell; others had taken part in small but well-organised raids on the coast of Occupied Europe. A force of Canadian and British troops had landed on the Norwegian coast, destroyed coal mines and burned oil stocks at Spitzbergen. Another, similar operation had been officially carried out at Vaagso, also in Norway. The first paratroop raid ever to be carried out by Britain had taken place the previous year in southern Italy and another in Northern France. All these had been conceived by the High

Command of the three services and carried out with the use of back-up forces only after meticulous preparation.

In general, however, it was a time when Britain was biding its time – gathering strength, building up forces and materials of war and only too pleased that Hitler was not attempting an invasion. Everyone in Britain was 'doing his or her bit', either in the Armed Forces or in civilian wartime organisations. Though anxious to see the war stepped up, everyone had to be patient.

But King and Cuthbertson, unwilling non-combatants, found it increasingly difficult to quell their impatience.

'Why the hell can't we be included in raids like those?' they asked each other, referring to the ones that *had* been launched on enemy territory.

Eventually their question became: 'Why don't we hear of more raids being carried out? Is nothing going to happen to get the bloody war moving?' Most Britons disliked the feeling that there was a prolonged lull, but few questioned the wisdom of the military and civil authorities, content to leave the running of the war to them.

'The CO won't give me a posting, but I'll never lie down to it,' Cuthbertson confided to King. 'I'll get out of this mob one way or another – even if I've to pretend to be a very bad dental mechanic.'

'Don't be a fool,' King exhorted him. 'You'll get nowhere doing that.' This was the responsible NCO talking, but also sympathising and trying to hold in check a wild streak that existed in his own mental make-up. He was not, as it turned out, to be able to do so in the circumstances in which he found himself as a sergeant in the Dental Corps. But he was trying.

They continued to watch the scene. Japan struck at Pearl Harbour. The United States shocked, came actively into the war.

'Now the Yanks will also see active service, but not us two,' they grumbled.

They began to give rein to their imagination by talking to each other of what they might have accomplished if only they had been allowed to transfer to a combatant unit. This led, eventually, to their considering some new way of throwing off the shackles they believed the Army had put on them.

'Is there anything we can do *on our own* to have a go at Jerry?' Cuthbertson asked as the two sat together one evening in King's private billet. It was a ridiculous, fanciful question. It was to prove a dangerous one also.

'Like what?' returned King, swiftly and sarcastically.

'Oh, I don't know, Peter. But surely there's *something* we can do instead of going to seed in this dump!'

'You're off your chump, Leslie. You've gone stark, raving mad.'

'No, I've not. I've been dreaming of something, trying to work out how it could be done. But it's ridiculous. I'm not daft – it wouldn't have a chance.'

'Come on – out with it,' ordered King.

'I was just wondering.'

'Well, wonder out loud.'

'Just wondering if it would be possible to make a private raid – not one organised by the Army – on France,' said Cuthbertson, and waited for the sergeant to blow his top.

King did not shout. He did not even smile.

'All right, Leslie, I'll tell you something now. I've been wracking my brains to think up some way to brighten up my war. I didn't quite think of that. I like it. Oh yes, I like it. But it's a ridiculous idea. Just plain bloody ludicrous.'

'But I wonder, Peter. Could it have just one chance in a thousand of coming off?'

'Not as much chance as snow in hell. What had you in mind, that you and I should just go off on the loose without a word to the Army, who'd stop us if they knew, and make a landing on the enemy coast? If we tried it, we'd be off our rockers. It just doesn't bear thinking about.'

But as they said goodnight, as King turned in to his bunk and Cuthbertson walked under the frosty February stars to his own billet, the idea stayed with them.

3 — The Plot Thickens

The thought of walking out of barracks and trying to raid France, without permission and in a private capacity, was so preposterous that they did not speak of it again for a week or so. They were not battle-trained. They had no combat experience, no resources. They would have no back-up assistance. The French coast would be strongly guarded. And there were a dozen more good reasons to place the idea in the realms of fantasy.

If either had been transferred at that stage to work by which they no longer came into contact with each other, there is little doubt that one of the most remarkable expeditions in that or any other war would never have taken place. But they were not separated and soon came round again to discussing the outrageous propostion, as though they were caught in the hands of fate, albeit a strange fate.

'Why aren't there any more raids on the enemy except by the RAF?'

That was the question that again lit the fuse of their 'impossible dream'. They could not know, of course, if anything of the sort was being mounted or not. Censorship was strict. They did not account for the possibility that perhaps Britain's High Command was pursuing a strategy which did not allow for such raids for the time being, and it was remarkable that two intelligent soldiers, one of them an NCO and a man some thirty years of age, failed to give enough thought to the possibility that a private raid such as they envisaged could upset some official military plan already in the pipeline.

Dreams of attempting a raid on their own initiative became more attractive as they moodily talked of the apparent stalemate in the prosecution of the war. They continued to debate the idea, in an academic sense to begin with.

'Could two men manage to approach the French coast

and gain a foothold unobserved?' they asked themselves.

'Could we even manage to leave Britain unobserved?'

'We'd need a rare stroke of luck.'

'There *is* such a thing as luck.'

They warmed to the subject. Their enthusiasm for the idea grew.

'*If* we were to attempt such a thing, how would we go about it?' was the next question.

Finally they began to draw up some details for a provisional plan. The meetings in the sergeant's billet became secret. Very secret.

The plan bore all the hallmarks of a Walter Mitty dream. Anyone listening to them as they plotted would have marked them down as successors to Don Quixote and Sancho Panza.

'I'm game to prepare for a raid,' decided King, 'with the proviso that we can duck out of it if we come to think it's just too mad.'

'I'm game too.'

They shook hands on the proposition.

First they began to compile a list of equipment they reckoned would be necessary to launch an unofficial and private invasion.

'We'll need some money,' said King. 'Nothing can be done without it. We'd need some to support ourselves between leaving barracks here and embarking in a boat. We'd probably require some to acquire a boat, to bribe someone to lend us one, for instance. How much money can you raise, Leslie?'

'I've got £15 in a bank up at Newcastle.'

'Would you be prepared to contribute that towards our expenses?'

'Yes, I can write to my mother enclosing a signed cheque and ask her to draw it from the bank and post it to me here.'

'Good man, Leslie. I'll match it with the same amount.'

Just £30 to mount a secret raid on German-held France! It was more than a trifle ridiculous. It would have cost the authorities a great deal more to send even two men, let alone a party of commandos, on a venture of that sort. To have one agent dropped by parachute by the RAF into France to link up with the French resistance movement was quite a costly affair by comparison.

The first list of 'essential' equipment they drew up consisted of two Service pistols plus ammunition; two bayonets; a quantity of hand-grenades; two entrenching tools; two pairs of small pliers; two pairs of large wire-cutters; haversacks and packs; two commando-type knives; one compass; shaving-gear; sewing-outfits for mending clothes; one clothes-brush for smartening soiled uniforms (they envisaged having to live rough while hiding before embarking from Britain); a spare uniform each and several pairs of boots. This represented a great deal of baggage to carry out of the barracks and to their point of embarkation, which should preferably be on the south coast. They deleted the spare uniforms and boots and considered that eventually other items would have to go too.

For the time being, they laid away the list in order to concentrate on something more important: there was no question of the Army training them for the expedition; this they must accomplish themselves. Realising that they must be as fit as possible and, more than that, tough, they drew up a programme by which they hoped to train themselves, physically at least, to a pitch as near to commando standards as they could reach – and this without anyone at the barracks guessing what they were about, or even wondering what they were up to.

It was essential, they realised, that their names should not be linked together in any way whatsoever. They must be seen in each other's company as little as possible. The training scheme they compiled would have to be executed, as far as they were able, at night-time, when there would be less chance of their being seen indulging in somewhat unusual activities. When Cuthbertson visited King's room in the evenings, he contrived to slip in unobserved.

After lights-out they donned physical-training clothes and left the barracks singly, meeting 400 yards away in a field. (There were no sentries posted at the gates of the dental unit building, only a system of scattered pickets being considered necessary.) From the field they ran for a number of miles every night. Gradually they stepped up the distances they covered – sometimes they kept going for five miles or more. On every occasion they made sure that they returned to the camp before reveille, passing through the gates individually.

Later they began running in denims and boots, later still wearing rather weighty packs on their backs, and steel helmets, and carrying rifles, again covering smaller distances at first and longer ones as time went on.

With growing physical fitness, and also because they now felt they were doing something practical and ambitious, their spirits greatly improved.

They practised crawling on their stomachs as soundlessly as they could, finding eventually that they could do so for upwards of an hour at a time with short rests without becoming too fatigued. The battledress uniforms they used for this became very soiled, but they were spare ones which King had managed to 'borrow' from stores, so they always had clean uniforms for wearing on duty and parades. For almost two months they trained in this way, often getting no more than an hour or two's sleep each night, sometimes arriving back at their billets with only time to wash themselves down before breakfast. Yet not once were they absent from or even late for duty.

Apart from training themselves, there were two further reasons for taking little sleep. First, they expected to be forced to go without sleep for long periods once they had launched themselves on their adventure. Secondly, it was also necessary to continue fulfilling their duties properly in order to avert suspicion. They tried to make up a little rest, however, by spending evenings lying on their beds before the night's training began.

On days when they were off-duty – and King arranged for these to coincide, they went on route-marches together, increasing the distance all the time until eventually they were covering some 20 miles carrying weighted haversacks and packs.

They knew little or nothing of any commando-type unarmed combat, but they invented, as best they could, methods of training themselves in this manner. They concentrated on wrestling with each other, trying to throw each other about and attempting to discover various holds which could not be broken. They also indulged in sessions of hitting and kicking each other in various parts of the body, with a real intention of hurting, because they considered it might be necessary during the type of venture they envisaged to endure pain with some stoicism. In addition, they agreed that there should be some effort to change and harden their personalities and mental outlook. Though their training programme was largely of a do-it-yourself character, they were making every effort to be as thorough as possible.

They did not overlook during their secret training the fact that they would need to become, if not crack-shots with a pistol, at least good ones. They were fortunate that King, himself a good shot with rifle and pistol, was not only drill sergeant but also small-arms instructor – an excellent one as it happened, and furthermore he was allowed to draw weapons from the armoury for demonstration and training provided he signed for them and returned them within a limit of time. Off-duty they spent many hours practising firing revolvers. Luckily the martial-minded Cuthbertson had in earlier years done much practising with an air-gun, and King had no novice on his hands. The sergeant found the young man an apt pupil with a pistol, and he brought his efficiency as a marksman to a degree almost as good as his own.

Fortune attended them in many ways during that time. It might have been thought that sooner or later, in spite of their precautions, some suspicion would have been aroused. At times it was impossible to leave the dental unit, or to return from what might appear to have been a run before breakfast, without being seen by someone or other. All that happened, however, was that they gained a name for being health fanatics.

Once only was there a danger of questions being asked. The incident occurred about a month after their training began.

King was keeping his soiled uniform, together with any of their plans that had been committtted to paper, under lock and key in a cupboard in his single-room billet. Cuthbertson, however, shared a room with some two dozen men. There was only a small locker beside his bed, but the sergeant had arranged for him to have the key to another, larger cupboard in this room.

It was a Friday evening, and a number of soldiers returned from spending an evening at a public house to find Cuthertson alone there and resting on his bed.

'Why don't you ever come out with us for a beer?'

'Aren't we good enough for you?'

'Some sort of snob or something?'

'You're just bloody unsociable.'

Cuthbertson tried to ignore the taunts. 'I'm a bit tired in the evenings. I don't drink anyway.'

'Milksop!'

His billet-mates then insinuated that he was getting preferential treatment.

'In what way?' Cuthbertson asked.

They told him. Was he the only man in the billet allowed to have an extra cupboard to himself? One that was also kept locked?

Tempers rose.

What was kept in the cupboard? What did he possess, they asked, that was so important that it must be kept under lock and key?

Cuthbertson got worried. The cupboard contained the soiled battledress and denims he used for night-training, items he was not entitled to possess. Behind the locked door lay also the £15 his mother had drawn from his bank, and a notebook containing some items he had jotted down and which he intended to bring to King's notice. One was: 'Water bottles in case no water available for a long period?' Another was: 'Some sort of medicines in case of illness caused by living rough?' The secret of the cupboard must, he was aware, be kept intact.

That night the hostility the others felt for the man who every evening went off by himself turned into open enmity.

'We can find out what's in that cupboard – with this, see?' One of the soldiers, a broad-shouldered private, produced a strong mess-knife. 'It won't take two ticks to force that door.'

As he moved towards the cupboard, Cuthbertson flung himself on the man. The struggle to preserve the secret of the cupboard developed into a fight.

The Geordie from Newcastle-upon-Tyne, a big chap and now very fit, was getting the better of his opponent when the billet-corporal entered the room. The door of the cupboard remained locked, but the corporal having stopped the fight, left saying he would report the incident.

Cuthbertson spent a worried night. The incidents leading to the fight would no doubt be revealed – and the cupboard opened.

4 — Preparations for Invasion

Fortunately it was to Sergeant King that the corporal's report was made, and the sergeant sent for the two pugilists.

Neither private blamed the other, but the question of the locked cupboard was mentioned. King gave them both a dressing-down, telling them there was to be no fighting, whatever the reason, and that any soldier who wished to make use of the cupboard might do so. It was never kept locked again, and afterwards Cuthbertson was careful what he placed in it. King did not, as anyone else to whom the fight was reported might have done, demand to see what the cupboard contained.

The incident turned out therefore to be of little consequence, apart from warning the would-be adventurers to be even more careful. More importantly, it made them aware how much they depended on each other. This was to be encouraged, in both their minds, for the more confidence they built up in each other, the better they would work as a team when the time came.

Nevertheless, their narrow escape from awkward questions startled them and gave them temporary second thoughts about the advisability of attempting such a self-imposed mission without any sort of permission. Recovering later from such fears, they joked with each other that if something did go wrong with their attempt, they would subsequently be muzzled like wild dogs by the authorities and confined to barracks for the duration. This led to their christening their forthcoming venture 'Operation Wild Dog'.

It also brought home to Cuthbertson that their prospective venture was the means of making him the lonelier of the two, as King fared better in the sergeants' mess.

By the end of March 1942, they believed they were sufficiently fit and self-trained to consider when and precisely how they would set about putting their ambitious scheme into operation. Additions were made to their original list of equipment, and they set about acquiring some of these. From the store-room in the school of dentistry they took, one article at a time, a pair of wire-cutters, a pair of pliers and two clothes-brushes, and from the barracks library maps of Cornwall and France and one showing the south of England, the Channel and the French coast, none of which was ever missed. They bought waterproof cases for the maps, a dozen boxes of matches, a quantity of soap, webbing-cleaner, blanco and two large tins of black boot polish. (Two soldiers who were smart and clean would invite less attention as they made their way to the south coast.) Similarly, it would be safer for two sergeants to be together, for if a search were mounted for them, it would be for a sergeant and a private. King decided to promote his companion unofficially, after they set off from Aldershot, and acquired a spare set of sergeant's stripes which, together with other articles, was locked away in the cupboard in his billet.

In the town of Aldershot they made friends with a group of Canadian soldiers and persuaded two of them to sell their commando-knives and entrenching tools. They were particularly pleased with these purchases.

Their preparations were extremely thorough. In case they suffered injury or wounding, they took from the stores, dressings, bandages, arm-slings and splints, to augment the 'first field dressing' sewn into all battledress uniforms. The large amount of soap they had bought was to help guard against disease, by cleanliness.

They even considered the possibility of having to drink impure water if by great fortune they got into France and had to hide out in the countryside. From the medical-room King picked up two small bottles of tablets designed to purify water which could not be boiled. A tablet from one bottle turned water green, and one from the other made it clear again and, in principle, safe for drinking.

Last but not least was the question of arms, ammunition and explosives. These being the most difficult items to acquire, and the more quickly missed, they postponed the attempt to 'borrow' them until the day before they would leave the unit to set off on their adventure. In the meantime they prepared for this with the same methodical care: King reckoned he could draw two revolvers from store, signing for them in the usual way, on the pretence that he wanted them for instruction purposes, the evening before they were to set out, and not be required to return them the same day. But acquiring hand-grenades would present a more difficult problem.

The sergeant arranged for Cuthbertson to be detailed from time to time for guard duties at the camp armoury, so that he could familiarise himself with the routine. The three guards had a break for a drink of cocoa half-way through the evening duty, for which they went into an adjoining room. This was the only time he might grab the explosives. Could he return to the room during this break without being asked by the other two guards why he had done so? On a number of separate evenings while on this duty he put it to the test, wandering into the armoury room and staying there alone while the other two sipped their cocoa. On one of these occasions he was asked, on rejoining the others, if he did not see enough of the armoury, and why did he not relax and take his drink while it was hot. His reply was that he was fascinated by arms and that he had never wished to be in the Dental Corps. This seemed to satisfy the others, who remarked that being in a medical unit was not a bad life, all things considered. When, on subsequent evenings, he left his cocoa to return to the armoury, no questions were asked of him, and he suggested to King that he make sure the same two men would be his guard companions on the night when he would attempt to take the grenades.

So far, so good. Moving-off day was fixed for 11 April. In order that they might have two clear days before being discovered missing after leaving Aldershot, King arranged for both of them to begin forty-eight hours' leave on the morning of that date and got passes signed by an officer. In addition, he stole a number of further pass-forms and railway-warrants, on which he put the official unit stamp, signed them with a 'W' followed by an indecipherable squiggle and then wrote the rank 'Capt'. These were then left blank for future use.

For the evening of 10 April, the day before their scheduled departure, King had Cuthbertson's name down for guard duty at the armoury, together with the two soldiers who laughingly called him 'gun mad'.

At 3 p.m. on that day King signed for and drew two .38 Colt revolvers from the storeroom, but two hours later, the weapons not having been returned, Private Heather, who was employed as a storeman, asked the sergeant what he had done with the weapons as they must be returned before he went off duty. King apologised, produced the pistols from his respirator haversack and watched Heather locking them up. This looked like the first piece of bad luck to interfere with 'Operation Wild Dog'.

Everything had been prepared for them to set out early the next day. To anyone's mind an attempted two-man raid on France with only pistols and knives as weapons and no back-up assistance would have seemed ridiculous in the extreme. To go without any firearms whatsoever (not that pistols were a great deal of use in the sort of emergencies envisaged), even the two quixotic hopefuls agreed would be farcical.

A little after 8 p.m. King went to the small-arms store, situated in a building known as 'the Maida School', with his respirator case slung over his shoulder, a groundsheet-cape over his arm and a screwdriver in his pocket. The building was empty except for a number of soldiers on fire-picket duty, and as he arrived, the pickets completed a patrol of the buildings and bade King good night before disappearing into a room for a break prior to making another tour of inspection. The door to the store was locked, and King worked on it with his screwdriver in full electric light, unable to switch it off in case he alerted the picket, whom he could plainly hear talking and laughing not far away. There was a sharp noise as the lock gave way, but no one came to investigate. Quickly he took two .38 revolvers in web holsters, placed them in his respirator case and left the room, wedging the door so that it did not stand ajar. He then made his way out of the building, acknowledging a greeting from a fire-picket returning there from the canteen.

He went to his billet, locked the weapons up in his cupboard and made his way immediately to the headquarters office. At the doorway he passed a picket in order to enter, but, being known to the soldier and because of his rank, he was not challenged.

Inside the office he made for the Dental Corps' sergeant-major's room, forced open a cupboard and took a box of .38 small arms ammunition. This also found its way swiftly into his own cupboard in his billet.

Sitting in his room, King was left to sweat it out in case anything went wrong with the part Cuthbertson was playing.

In the armoury Cuthbertson waited nervously for the evening break. When it came, he took a couple of sips at his cocoa and moved towards the room where the arms were kept – to some banter from his two fellow-guards, who said someone should give him a couple of field-guns for Christmas.

Inside the room, Cuthbertson pushed the door to quietly but did not actually close it. He was so nervous that he had to compose himself for half a minute before beginning to force open the cupboard door. As the lock gave, he forced a loud cough, hoping grimly that nothing had been heard by the others. Putting his hand inside, he began to place hand-grenades in his respirator haversack, which was slung over his shoulder and from which he had previously extracted the gas-mask and placed pieces of cardboard to make it appear square and bulky. One of them began to roll towards the edge of the shelf, but he caught it in time. When the haversack was full, he closed the cupboard door and rejoined his companions, humming a tune and pretending to appear at ease.

The remainder of that spell of guard duty passed uneventfully, though somewhat anxiously, for Cuthbertson. He went to King's billet at the double and unloaded his respirator haversack. He had managed to acquire half-a-dozen grenades.

There were several anxious hours to spend wondering if

the theft of the guns and grenades would be discovered too soon, and if anything else might occur to prevent their leaving the barracks the next morning.

Apart from the uniform Cuthbertson wore, everything he would take was now in King's room. The remainder of his gear he had already put into his kitbag, which he left in his billet with a note inside addressed to the quartermaster-sergeant stating: 'These items should be put in the company store.' At the end of this message he had scrawled three words from a popular song of the time: 'We'll meet again.' King also left spare items in a kitbag with a similar note.

But there were some last-minute tasks: fixing rubber soles to their boots (to help silence in movement, which they envisaged, might be essential at times in the future); burning lists and notes referring to the venture, wrappings, paper from stolen articles and any personal letters they had in their pockets, and scrubbing out King's billet to leave it clean and tidy.

Had they not occupied their waiting time in this manner, it is just possible that at this eleventh hour they might have called off the wild scheme which they had approached with such an odd mixture of a loyal desire to help the war effort, romantic belief in their capacity to defy the immense odds against them and great attention to detail.

Records of their preparations were kept meticulously. King even placed in his pocket a note bearing numbers of the two stolen pistols – 645161 and 648440.

They decided that two of the more weighty articles, the bayonets and entrenching tools, could not be taken. Everything else from their secret cache in the cupboard was placed in their haversacks, packs and pockets.

Nothing more remained to be done, apart from reaffirming their commitment to the venture and to each other, before the time came, at 5.30 a.m., when they hoped to make their way separately to the barrack gates, pass out and meet some distance down the road to begin their adventure.

5 — Alerting the PM!

By luck rather than conscious thought the time chosen for setting off was in their favour. Had they continued their training much longer, they might well have become bored with it; had they gone on for a few more weeks with anxiety about their plans being uncovered, they might have considered the attempt not worthwhile. By the law of averages they were due for some hitch in their run of good luck, and if they had waited much longer and this had occurred, they might have cancelled altogether an operation from which success must hang by such a slender thread.

As they stood in King's room for a few minutes before 5.30 a.m., they shook hands but found conversation difficult. King went first, sauntering along to the barracks entrance and passing through. Cuthbertson waited anxiously for a few minutes and then followed suit. It was a clear, calm morning with no sound but the birds' chorus and the dull tread of his boots, despite the new rubber soles.

The parade-ground was silent and empty. The barracks was not yet astir, but one man, no doubt a night-picket returning to his billet after duty, passed by and shouted a greeting to Cuthbertson, who quickened his pace towards the exit. He caught up with King, and they marched together for a time towards the railway station without speaking – as far as Aldershot Barracks or any passer-by was concerned, two soldiers going on weekend leave.

Their programme for the next two days was, of course, carefully worked out. First they were to go to London, then on to Cornwall, with which county King said he was fairly familiar. The train on which they intended to travel was scheduled to leave Aldershot at a time soon after they arrived at the station. To leave the barracks at 5.30 meant that they would not have long to wait before boarding the train, thus leaving little time for the RTO staff at the station, or military police on duty there, to take a great deal of interest in them.

To a discerning eye they may not have presented an altogether unusual appearance, though they were a trifle overloaded to be going on leave, having heavy packs, surmounted by rolled groundsheets, bulky haversacks and bulging pockets. Their leave-passes were in order, but their travel-warrants were forged. Military police were often to be found at railway stations inspecting leave-passes and on the look-out for anything they considered they should report concerning travelling soldiers. The two hopefuls had no wish to be obliged even to pass the time of day with anyone from that corps. If by any chance they had been asked to turn out their packs, the discovery of arms, ammunition and grenades would have presented the authorities with an intriguing situation.

Soon, however, they were in the train, with a compartment to themselves, rattling towards London.

They discussed their plans further. They aimed to lose no time in London taking another train to the West Country and reaching Cornwall before their forty-eight hours' leave ended. Once there they would not at once seek to cross to France but instead spend several weeks on yet another phase of self-training – learning to hide out in open ground and subsisting only on food that the countryside might offer. This would, they hoped, include any vegetables that might grow in farm fields, berries from trees and such like, drinking-water from streams and places where rain-water collected. They would experiment eating anything growing that they might consider edible and discover what they could consume without making themselves feel sick or ill.

Within a few days they would be posted as absent without leave, and the theft of arms and ammunition would be discovered. Civil and military police would be alerted to keep a look out for them, and it would be altogether inadvisable to attempt to gain a cooked meal or even to enter a village to buy food. If not before, then certainly now, they were very much on their own.

The hurdles they still had to clear, even in relation to getting out of the country, looked larger now than before they had set off. Could they succeed in acquiring a boat, not a large one but suitable for crossing the Channel? If they did, could they sail it? King had handled a small sailing-boat a few times, but never one with a motor. All Cuthbertson had done in that sphere was to row a boat. Neither had ever ventured in this manner more than hailing distance from the shore; such sailing had been restricted to holiday jaunts and had required no knowledge of navigation. Both knew something about petrol-engines, but only in an amateur way.

Again, if they did acquire a boat, would there not be wartime restrictions on sailing away from Britain?

They were questions which might have daunted many men and led them even at that stage to cancel the operation they planned so optimistically.

At the London terminus they passed successfully through the barrier from the platform at which the train had come in, but as they loitered in the station hall, waiting for the Plymouth train they hoped to board, a military policeman approached them. He asked where they were going, and they said they were on their way to Cornwall on leave. They were requested to produce their leave-passes, which of course showed their names, and as they handed them over, they were extremely anxious.

The policeman returned the passes. 'They seem to be in order,' he said.

The two began to move off.

'Just a minute. Come back here.'

What had gone wrong?

'A bit unusual for a sergeant and a private to be going on leave together, isn't it?' suggested the military policeman.

The set of stolen sergeant's stripes had not yet been stitched to Cuthbertson's sleeves. They couldn't be because his pass showed him as a private.

King had visualised this possibility during the forty-eight hours their passes covered. He had an answer ready, but a little play-acting was also needed. 'It would seem a bit odd to you, of course,' he said, trying to appear frank and at ease. 'We're in the same corps, but we're also cousins. It might be a long time, with this lousy war in progress, before we can spend another leave together.'

The policeman did not answer at once. His eyes devoured them confidently from head to toe. 'All right, proceed,' he said at last.

There followed an uncomfortable wait of upwards of an hour before they could pass through the barrier to the platform from which the Plymouth train would pull out. They spent the time in a station buffet drinking hot tea and buying a large bag of buns and cakes to take with them on their journey. This caused them some concern, as plenty of military police would be on duty at Plymouth and no doubt at other stations *en route*.

They spent most of the journey in silence. Cuthbertson took a pipe and tobacco from a pocket and commenced priming and lighting it. Neither was a smoker (nor did they drink alcohol), and the young man's efforts with his pipe were unsatisfactory. He had bought it because an idea had entered his head that a man with a pipe stuck in his mouth gave an impression of being contented and therefore innocent, and he reckoned there might be times when they would have to appear so.

They were, however, to meet no further interrogation on that journey. At Plymouth they passed out of the station without incident and made their way into the town, where they hoped to spend one last night in a boarding-house with cooked food and a bed before their leave-passes expired. Then they would take to living rough and hiding in open country.

Their customary caution prompted them to choose a boarding-house that lay in a street well behind the sea-front, and when they had booked a room for the coming night, that of 11–12 April, they retired to it at once with the intention of not leaving the house until the next day.

This exceptional prudence did not altogether accord with what might have been expected of men engaged on such a madcap operation. On the other hand, their extreme care had no doubt helped materially to keep their secret safe thus far; and certainly it revealed that they viewed their attempt seriously, even if more than a shade too optimistically.

Their behaviour was more in line with escaped prisoners-of-war trying to make their way home through enemy territory than with members of the usually peaceful Army Dental Corps in their own country and ostensibly on leave. They were, of course, anxious that nothing should occur to prevent their attempt to make a raid on France. If they were discovered before they managed to leave Britain, their explanation as to their real intentions would, moreover, be treated as an unlikely tale, and punishment would no doubt swiftly follow.

When the landlady knocked on their door to inform them that the evening meal was ready, they had no wish to show themselves to others in the dining-room and made the excuse that they were not feeling too well, being, as they said, exceptionally tired after an army exercise which had preceded the start of their leave – despite the fact that they were ravenous for food. The statement about the 'exercise' and consequent 'fatigue' was not in any sense untrue, though they failed to mention that it was self-imposed. Indeed an interesting feature throughout their operation was the number of times they told the truth, a prime example of which was to occur later that evening when together they composed a letter which was an inspired, if somewhat astounding, part of their preparations.

They were relieved when the landlady insisted that they must not go without a meal and offered to bring their food up to their room on a tray, waving aside their fears that this would put her to too much trouble. As it happened, the dining-room was by no means crowded. In the spring of 1942 few people in Britain were in the mood to take a holiday or able to do so, the war-effort on the civilian as well as the military side being very much in top gear.

Their desire to maintain secrecy prompted them to place the regulations 'black-outs', precautions against enemy air-raids, on the windows and draw the curtains earlier than might have been necessary, and after their hot meal and a short rest they again busied themselves with what they believed were necessary tasks. First King produced the spare set of sergeant's stripes he had acquired, and Cuthbertson sewed them on the tunic of his battledress.

Then they settled down together to compose, very carefully, a letter to – of all people – the Prime Minister, Mr Winston Churchill!

This was the final draft of what they wrote, penned by King in a neat and precise hand and addressed to the Prime Minister:

7536394 Sgt. P. King,
AD Corps School of Instruction,
Campbell Road,
Aldershot.

Sir,

I trust you will pardon the liberty I take in writing to you, but I feel that it is necessary in this case to go a little outside the 'usual channels' and make my report to you direct.

I am an 'A 1' soldier, with no relatives or dependants, and very anxious to do something really active in this war, and although I have made several applications, I am still wasting my time in a non-combatant unit.

Consequently I have made plans to 'have a go' at the Boche myself, and when you receive this I shall have left the country three days and, I hope, safely landed on the coast of Occupied France. I believe that two men can enter that country unperceived, whereas hundreds of Commandos with all that goes with them would easily be detected, and I intend to stay there three months, inflicting as much damage to the enemy as is humanly possible. My objects are:

I. To Destroy, by fire or other means, important buildings, bridges, vehicles, rail-tracks, weapons, aerodromes, equipment, etc, etc.
II. TO Destroy and Disorganise communications, power, food and supply services.
III. To Destroy as many Nazis and Quislings as possible.
IV. To help the RAF by means of fires and morse messages. Signal 'KC'.
V. To bring back information regarding invasion preparations etc.

TARGET: Fifty Nazis and £50,000 worth of damage. My only regret is that whilst fighting as hard as anyone in this war for my country, I shall no doubt be posted, INCORRECTLY, as a deserter, and I appeal to you, Sir, to use your influence and understanding to post me as on a 'Special Mission' or something of the sort.

No. 10511436 Pte L. Cuthbertson of the AD Corps, Aldershot, is in the same position as myself and feels the way I do, therefore I have decided to take him with me, as two can be far more efficient than one with no extra risk. We are properly armed and equipped and will live 'on the land'.

I thank you, Sir, for your indulgence, and do hope you will help us in this matter of 'postings'.

I am, sir,
Your obedient servant,
P. King, sgt.

It was certainly a remarkable letter. Few outside the country's High Command would have contacted the war-leader, let alone a sergeant and a private. In addition, its content was fantastic, the detailed plan being ambitious beyond credibility.

For two men, armed with revolvers and half a dozen hand-grenades, to effect such death and destruction, even if they managed to leave Britain and land in France, might have appeared, even in their quixotic hopes, quite impossible. Perhaps if they managed to link up with the French resistance movement or British saboteurs officially parachuted into France, they might stand a chance – but not on their own. The letter was no doubt born of a feeling of 'in for a lamb, in for a sheep'.

Apart from their unquenchable desire for action and to make a total contribution to the war-effort, albeit an irresponsible one, there was a feeling at the back of their minds that some incidents in war had been stranger than fiction. If they were to succeed only partially, it would, however, be very strange indeed.

They placed the letter – together with their Army Pay Books 64, which were proof of their identities – in an envelope addressed to the Prime Minister, No. 10, Downing Street, London. This in turn was placed in a larger envelope which they addressed to 'The Chief Postmaster, Edinburgh', and included a letter requesting that the enclosed envelope be kept for a couple of days and then put in the post to Mr Churchill, as 'it was vital to the war effort'. Their intention was to post the letter immediately prior to their leaving for France. If, as they believed, a search for them would soon begin, they had no wish for it to be intensified by startling the authorities too early in their game.

That night Cuthbertson wrote another and personal letter, which he intended to post at the same time. This was to his mother at 226 Helmsley Road, Newcastle-upon-Tyne, and it stated:

'I am going overseas on a secret mission for my country.

'There are lots of things I should like to explain, but I must wait until I see you again. I can tell you that if I do get home safely, and everything turns out as I expect it will, you will be the proudest mother in the whole world.'

King wrote no personal letters. He stated in the letter to Downing Street that he 'had no dependants', and he had told his comrade in the operation that he had 'no near relatives'. This, and a statement that the sergeant wanted to live in New Zealand when the war was over, was all that Cuthbertson knew about King's background. Despite their friendship, Cuthbertson was conscious of the other's superior rank, and though he spoke often about his own private life before joining the Army, he asked no questions concerning that of King.

They awoke the next morning refreshed and hopeful. As they were about to move on, they risked taking breakfast in the dining-room, then paid their bill, shouldered their packs and haversacks and left the boarding-house.

In about twenty-four hours their leave-passes would run out, and they would be posted as absent without leave. But though they had not yet dropped the letter to the Prime Minister into a postbox, the writing of it, they felt, had set the seal on their adventure.

They set off from Plymouth to make their way, by map and on foot, avoiding roads and towns, to the Cornish coast area near the River Fowey, a place at which King had spent several holidays, some twenty-four miles as the crow flies but a much greater distance the way they would have to go.

They were to sleep in no bed and eat no good meal for some weeks, a period that was to prove remarkable for two non-combatants with a taste for adventure.

6 — Nearly Caught Out

Their plan being to remain in Cornwall for several weeks and keep to the countryside, where it was unlikely they would meet either civilian or military police, they made no effort to break any records with their first day's march. If they reached the Looe area, on the coast and more than half-way to Fowey, before the light faded, when they would have to search for a place to sleep, they would be well satisfied.

They allowed themselves a guarded feeling of freedom, the first since their plan had been conceived and begun. This, together with a sense of having set off at last on the first leg of their adventure, put them in good spirits, and they enjoyed the fresh sea-breezes and burgeoning of spring on the Cornish headlands.

From the point of view of 'living off the land', it might not have been the best season for finding a rich growth of vegetables in farm fields or edible berries on bushes and trees, but it was not the worst from the point of view of living rough seriously affecting their health and constitution. They felt they could rely on spring cabbage, some early lettuce and perhaps radishes being available to be taken by stealth, stored in some hideout and eaten raw. Some of Cuthbertson's uncles in the north-east were keen gardeners and allotment owners, and he remembered being told that spinach and spinach beet could be sown at summer's end to stand the winter, and that broad beans planted in November would come through all but the hardest winter, so perhaps they could find some of those, too, to augment their diet. In addition, they had already planned to experiment by eating other growing things – even grass, they suggested.

When they halted for lunch, however, they did not search for any food of that nature but ate instead a few stale items left over from the bag of cakes and buns they had bought at the railway terminus in London.

In the evening they climbed down on to a beach and searched for a sheltered place well above the high-water mark. They found a cave, and there they remained for the night, sleeping rolled up in a groundsheet.

Before nightfall on the second day they reached the vicinity of Polruan, and between there and Fowey, at a spot they later learned was named Pencarrow Head, they found another cave in a small, deserted cove. This one was completely out of sight from the cliff-tops and even from the sea, for to find it one had to make one's way some distance inside a long, narrow fissure cutting into the cliff face. There was not a great deal of light in the cave, even during the day, for it was entered through a narrow opening, but it was dry and shielded from the sea winds. More important, it was a cave which would take a fair amount of finding for any who did not know of its existence, and they decided to make it their headquarters. In it they stowed their packs, haversacks and other baggage, concealing them under piles of stone, so that during the days that were to follow they would not be carrying about their persons pistols, grenades, compass and maps, which would be suspicious articles if discovered.

The next day they spent reconnoitring nearby fishing-villages, Polperro, Polruan, Fowey and others, and were delighted to discover, as King had promised, boats of all sizes and types drawn up on the beaches.

They talked to a ferryman in one of these places, posing as soldiers on leave, and inquired as to the possibility of hiring a boat to do some fishing. The conversation brought them face-to-face with what looked like the first real obstacle to their plans: the ferryman was of the opinion that not many, if any, boat-owners would be prepared to hire out any of their craft. Wartime regulations, he added, forbade any person taking a boat further out than two miles, and, furthermore, coastguard and naval stations along the coast kept a day-and-night watch to make sure no one did! Following this information they were a little depressed for a time, and even questioned the possibility that their plans to cross the Channel to France might come to nothing in the end.

It was one of several times when they were tempted to give up, report back to the Army and take their punishment for being absent without leave. Despite their earnest and serious desire to make a dramatic contribution to the war effort, and the somewhat romantic military streak that existed in their minds, they were both highly intelligent, and their common sense reminded them constantly of the serious dangers to which they would expose themselves if they had the good fortune actually to embark on the venture. Though it was always a likelihood that they would cancel the raid they envisaged, it says a great deal for their courage that they continued undaunted.

Faced with this snag, they decided to put it in the back of their minds for the time being while they continued training themselves. They perceived that, if they reached the French coast, they might well have a high cliff to scale, and in various secluded coves they set about practising climbing some of the steep and sometimes sheer cliffs. In the more dangerous spots they roped themselves together, and as time went on, they found they could tackle steep ascents with some confidence and speed. They also continued crawling-practice at night, and found they could move rather well in this fashion and with less and less fatigue.

The first day they came across a field which they guessed was owned by a market-gardener and in which were spring cabbage and lettuce. No one was about to see them, and they pulled a couple of cabbages and some lettuces and beat a hasty retreat from the area. When they found a stream, they drank water from it, cleaned their stolen vegetables, ate some and took the remainder to their cave. That night they returned and filled haversacks and packs with more vegetables.

Later they found a hen-pen, to which they returned at night-time taking a number of eggs back to the cave. They ate one a day so long as they lasted, Cuthbertson finding them distasteful raw but swallowing them in order to gain nourishment. Another night they raided a farm shed which held a store of turnips and potatoes and took a quantity of each to eat raw. In this way they subsisted quite well for a time, though sometimes they were so hungry that they almost risked entering a café for a meal. Once or twice after the first week they did buy some buns and apples, waiting for a village shop to have no other customers in it before one of them made the purchase.

For the sake of experiment they tried to eat both grass and seaweed, neither of which they could swallow after chewing. Sometimes they suffered from diarrhoea, which they were certain was caused by their diet.

On one occasion, while loitering near the outskirts of Polperro, they chatted to a boy who offered them sweets from a paper bag. They offered to buy these from the lad, who accepted a shilling, three times what he had himself paid for them, and he watched open-eyed as the two soldiers demolished the contents of the bag in record time.

The youngster, who confided that he wanted to be a soldier when he grew up, was plainly fascinated by the two sergeants, who told him they were on leave and staying at a village 'about five miles away'. When the soldiers said they must be on their way, the boy asked if they might be at the same place the next day so that he could talk to them again. Considering that the little fellow could bring them no harm, they agreed to be there at the same time the next day, on condition, they added jocularly, that he brought with him another bag of toffees and some cakes or buns. A half-crown changed hands, and the boy sped off.

The next day they again met the boy, who had made the purchases required of him, and he received another half-crown for himself.

It appeared that he did not live in Polperro but at a solitary cottage near a wood a short distance away, and when he urged them to go with him to meet his mother, the two fugitives decided there might not be a great deal of risk in doing so, despite their rule to keep away from towns and people.

The boy's mother welcomed them into her house and offered them a portion of huge rice pudding she had just baked. Starved of cooked food, they found it delicious and did not fail to tell her so, whereupon they were urged to finish the bowl between them. They left with a huge paper bag of fruit cake presented to them by their hostess, which helped them to view the next day's raw cabbage with greater stoicism, for they would not risk another visit to their benefactor.

As they continued to live like fugitives in their own country, Cuthbertson, more than King, who had no close relatives, was liable to suffer a temporary weakening of resolution. He thought of home, of his family and of his sweetheart, May Forster, who, like him, was nineteen years of age. He had written a letter to his mother (not yet posted), but he would not write to May because he considered too many letters might be dangerous.

He realised that by then the civilian police at Newcastle would have been contacted by the military authorities and asked to call at his home. Discovering he was not there, the police would no doubt inform his parents that he was absent without leave and ask them if they had heard from their son since 11 April. What, he asked himself, would his family – and May – be thinking about him? They would no doubt be both perplexed and worried. He was not a little concerned about this, and looked forward to the time when he could post his letter. He hoped that when it was delivered in Newcastle they would, if nothing else, be assured that he was neither a criminal nor a bad soldier. In the meantime, however, he was prey to many disturbing thoughts.

One morning, after breakfasting on lettuce and raw potatoes from their little store of food, they went out of the cave for a stroll. It was a beautiful sunny morning, with a light breeze from the sea, and the beach of the little cove was deserted and intensely peaceful.

But round the curve of the headland, high above them and some distance away, appeared two figures in dark uniform. The men on the headland began to wave, and it was obvious to King and Cuthbertson that they had been spotted. If they doubled back to the cave, they would be seen, and their hideout no doubt discovered. They returned the wave and walked on.

Instead of passing on along the headland above them, the newcomers began to make their way down into the cove, as if to intercept the two on the beach. Soon the latter were relieved to see that they were not police, but then they recognised them as naval petty-officers and were assailed by fresh and imaginative doubts. Was it possible, for instance, that coastal naval stations had been asked to look out for two soldiers from the Dental Corps who were now very much absent without leave and might be suspected of stealing a couple of Service pistols?

The two soldiers leaned against a boulder, attempting to appear calm and unconcerned. Cuthbertson took his pipe from his pocket and handed it to King, who put it unprimed into his mouth. The younger man thought it made him look contented, but he was far from that.

When the naval men came up to them, King took the initiative, thinking that attack was perhaps the best form of defence, saying it was a fine morning and asking if they were on leave or off duty. The naval men's reply was that they were not on leave, and why did the sergeant ask the question? Because, answered King, *they* were on leave. One of the petty-officers then cheerfully complimented the soldiers on their luck to be off duty and said that he and his companion were from a nearby naval station and were on patrol. For a time afterwards the hopeful adventurers' feeling of insecurity was heightened. Seldom had two soldiers, more than willing to fight, and guilty of deserting their posts for a loyal reason, felt like criminals. For several days they stayed in the cave during the hours of daylight and did not venture far during their night-training exercises.

Though the meeting with the petty-officers had produced no unlucky complications, another incident was to prove more alarming. In order to keep themselves in trim, they decided one night to take a long route-march using the country roads in order to make better headway. It was a dark, rather still night with plenty of cloud in the sky. There would be little or no traffic on the roads, which they planned to leave smartly if they heard a vehicle moving. They were some eight miles from the cave, thinking of turning about, marching a stretch of road darkened by surrounding trees, when there was a gleam a few paces ahead and a sudden shout. Taken completely by surprise, they were unaware which they were conscious of first, the sight of a rifle and bayonet or the challenge.

'Halt, who goes there?' It was a familiar warning, given in a Cornish accent.

They obeyed the command and were surrounded by more figures with rifles and bayonets.

'Who the hell are you?' asked King.

'The Home Guard,' came the reply.

It was incredible, they told themselves, that despite their supreme caution they had walked right into a patrol – and a Home Guard one at that.

King greeted them in as cheerful a voice as he could muster. They were friends, he said, certainly not enemy invaders, if that was what they thought. Army actually. Sergeants. *Regulars*. In his most authoritative drill-sergeant manner he added that he was pleased to see that the Home Guard was on its toes.

'Good lads,' put in Cuthbertson. 'You're doing a great job.'

The man who had challenged them, a private, admitted that the Home Guard did try to do a good job, respectfully adding the word 'sergeant', to which Cuthbertson was not, of course, entitled.

That, however, was not the end of the matter. The private asked what they were doing on the road at this time of night.

'On leave,' snapped King.

The group of Home Guard men held a hasty consultation and then apologetically informed the two that they must be taken to their officer. They were marched off and presented to a middle-aged Home Guard lieutenant, who they imagined might be a little diffident as to how much authority he had over two regular Army sergeants. Being informed that his 'prisoners' were on leave, he told them politely that he must be satisfied this was so and requested they show their leave-passes.

For less meticulous planners the game would no doubt have been up, but their unusual care and caution was to pay off once again: since their passes had expired, they had made out others every two days from their supply of forms with forged authorisation. Each produced a 'current' pass.

The officer scrutinised them, appeared to find them in order and handed them back, but not without remarking that it seemed somewhat strange for two men on leave to be strolling about in the middle of the night.

Anxious to be off, the Dental Corps men accorded the Home Guard officer a smart salute and marched away, but not without a number of misgivings. Though they had written fictitious names on the documents and been careful to give both the rank of sergeant, the passes bore the stamp of the Army Dental Corps at Aldershot.

Was there any chance that the incident would prove unfortunate? They feared that by then information would have been widely relayed that two Dental Corps men from Aldershot were on the run. Would the Home Guard lieutenant hear of it and remember them? Or would he talk of the incident and be told that information was required of two soldiers who might answer their descriptions?

They could only hope that neither of these eventualities would take place.

7—The Birds Have Flown

Meanwhile, certain discoveries at Aldershot had caused a stir. The first sign that all was not in order at the Dental Corps unit had made its appearance on the morning of Sunday 12 April some twenty-nine hours after the two over-enthusiastic soldiers had gone on leave. It was at that time discovered that a door and two cupboards had been forced and that arms and ammunition had disappeared. A thorough search failed to produce the missing items.

By next day suspicion rested on King and Cuthbertson. All other soldiers who had been on week-end leave had returned to barracks except them. The two were posted absent without leave; the civil police notified and the military police informed of the missing weapons.

Corporal J. J. Murphy and Lance-Corporal W. Gunston, of the Corps of Military Police, arrived at the barracks on 13 April to investigate.

They were told that between 5 p.m. on the 10th and 10.15 a.m. on the 12th two .38 Colt pistols contained in web holsters had been taken from a store-room in the Maida School at the Dental Corps centre, the door having been forced open, and that 'a similar crime' had been committed in the office of Regimental-Sergeant-Major E. C. Duddridge, forty-one rounds of .38 small arms ammunition having disappeared.

The two military policemen made investigations and sent a report to the Assistant Provost Marshal of the Aldershot District, in which they stated that their enquiries had revealed that Sergeant King was known to have taken two pistols from the store on the 10th, but that, as it was part of his duty to instruct recruits in weapon-training, nothing unusual had then been suspected. Later, those weapons had in fact been returned to the store. Sergeant King had, however, been seen that evening in the Maida School by the picket, but as he was a member of the staff his visit was not questioned.

The report continued:

> Sergeant King, during his presence at the dental centre, formed a friendship with a recruit, No. 10511436 Private Leslie Cuthbertson, who is absent without leave, and it is believed that he went away with Sergeant King. Both these soldiers were known to be dissatisfied with the lack of excitement in their unit and had expressed their desire for a transfer to the commandos.
>
> Sergeant King's bunk has been searched, and it would appear from the condition of the interior that his action was premeditated. A search of his personal kit failed to reveal anything which might assist us in tracing his whereabouts. As a complete uniform and respirator were left in the bunk, it is believed that he may be wearing civilian clothes.
>
> The only description of him which is available is as follows: age twenty-seven (looks older); height 5 feet 10 inches; weight 184½ lbs; scar on back of right shoulder, flat feet. Believed to have tattoo marks 'Please' and 'Thank you' on the palms of his hands.

No one at the barracks knew that the two missing soldiers had two uniforms. It is interesting to note that, following the report from the two military police investigators, a watch was kept for two men in civilian clothes, almost certainly for King dressed in that way.

The report added:

> The search for Cuthbertson's kit did not reveal anything which would assist us in our enquiry. He is described as follows: age nineteen years; weight 159 lbs; hair brown, eyes blue, fresh complexion. No distinguishing marks.
>
> We ascertained that King's home was in New Zealand, and that he was in the habit of spending his privilege leaves at Coombe Martin, North Devon, where the civilian police have been asked to keep watch.
>
> The circumstances pertaining to this crime leave little doubt as to the culprits. Only a member of the staff could gain admittance to the respective places without being challenged.

There was no mention in the report of compass, maps, water-purification pills and other items taken by King and Cuthbertson, and apparently these were not missed. The letter to the Prime Minister not having been posted as yet, all that was known was that two soldiers were absent without leave and that two pistols, together with ammunition, had been stolen.

The commander of the Farnborough sub-area ordered that a court of enquiry be held to investigate the loss of the arms and ammunition. This took place at the Army Dental Corps's School of Instruction on 18 April, before Major R. L. Blackborow, Royal Army Service Corps, Captain H. Roden, Royal Army Service Corps, and Second-Lieutenant J. W. Shaw, Royal Engineers.

The first witness was Private E. W. Heather, of the Army Dental Corps, who stated that on 10 April he had obtained the key to the arms store from RSM Duddridge for the purpose of cleaning revolvers. At about 14.30 hours he finished this job and locked up the store. At 15.00 hours Sergeant King asked him for the key of the arms store in order that he might obtain revolvers to show his recruits.

Later, at about 16.30 hours, witness again met Sergeant King, who was proceeding in the direction of the arms store. He returned the key to witness, who visited the store to ascertain if all the revolvers were present. Two were missing, and Heather went to Sergeant King and asked him what he had done with the two revolvers he had been using. The sergeant made apologies and produced the two revolvers from his respirator haversack. These Private Heather replaced in their holsters in the arms store; then he locked up and returned the key to Sergeant-Major Duddridge.

Witness added that he did not sleep in the arms store but on the ground floor of the building in which it was situated. Apart from the normal picket, Sergeant King was the only person he saw in that building on the evening of 10 April.

Another witness, Private G. J. D. Donovan, told the court that on that evening, at about 18.00 hours, he had entered the building to carry out duties with the fire-picket. At 19.30 hours he left the building to have supper and returned at about 20.15 hours to the front entrance, where he saw Sergeant King, who soon afterwards entered the building. At about 20.45 hours Sergeant King left the building, and witness saw that he was carrying his respirator, which was partially concealed by a raincoat over one of his arms.

Discovery of the theft was made by RSM Duddridge who told the enquiry that at about 10.15 hours on Sunday 12 April he had had occasion to enter the small-arms store, when he found that the key would not turn properly in the lock. Eventually he found that the door had been forced and wedged with a wad of paper to prevent its opening. He checked the revolvers and found two missing, together with holsters. The RSM said that he had telephoned Major Mackie, of the Army Dental Corps, and informed him of his discovery; later the military police were contacted. The missing revolvers led him, stated the sergeant-major, to check on the ammunition which was kept in his office. He found that forty-one rounds of .38 pistol ammunition were also missing. The military police arrived, investigated the loss of the weapons and then found that the door of the ammunition cupboard had been forced and evidently re-closed without damaging the lock. RSM Duddridge added that he had last checked the revolver ammunition on 7 April and found it to be correct.

Questioning of the picket on duty at the headquarters office on 10 and 11 April was fruitless, though there were men on duty at the building which housed the arms store and also at the headquarters office both day and night.

To add to what still remained a mystery, it was stated by another witness, Private C. E. Leader, that on the afternoon of 10 April, the day the two revolvers were borrowed from the store by King, the sergeant did not give weapon-instruction, and none was shown to his squad of recruits.

Forwarding the evidence that had been taken to the commander of the area, Lieutenant-Colonel S. H. Woods, commandant of the School of Instruction at the Dental Corps, stated that the court of enquiry had recorded no opinion regarding the loss of the pistols and ammunition, but wrote that it was his own opinion, and that of the military and civil police, that the stolen articles had been taken by Sergeant King, 'who has not been seen since and has now been posted as a deserter'.

At this stage it was not much more than a case of two men being posted absent without leave, a posting the two renegades dearly hoped would be altered when their letter reached the Prime Minister.

If they were the men who had taken the pistols – and

there was little doubt in the minds of the officers at the dental centre, then there was no suggestion of what use they intended to make of the weapons. Even though it was known that both hankered after military action, an adventure such as the two were planning was not at that time envisaged by anyone in authority in the Aldershot district.

The CO of the dental unit recalled that Sergeant King had several times applied to be transferred to a combatant unit, and remembered that it was King himself who had more recently brought Cuthbertson before him with a similar request. He felt sure that it was they who had taken the weapons, and he visualised them somewhere in Britain, unwilling to return to duty, carrying pistols about with them and perhaps practising shooting with them. But if anyone had put forward a theory that the two men under his command were actually planning a raid on the enemy, he would have dismissed the suggestion as bizarre in the extreme.

For the time being, the investigation was to remain at a local level.

8 — On The Run

At that time King and Cuthbertson had been on the run for ten days without finding any means of getting to France, but their encounter with the Home Guard patrol caused them to view this matter with more urgency.

The following day they risked paying a visit during the daytime to the waterfront at Fowey, and sought out the ferryman from whom they had tried to hire a boat. They repeated their wish, and after some conversation he admitted reluctantly that he knew where he could lay his hands on a small boat with an engine. But he was extremely doubtful that he could lend it to them.

The next day, however, they returned and attempted to ingratiate themselves with him. They mentioned that they were on leave with plenty of money and could pay well for the hire of a boat. The ferryman remained convinced that he should not accede to their wish.

Under cover of night they visited a number of motor-car petrol-stations and were fortunate enough to find a few cans of petrol that had not been locked away. These they took to their cave.

On the night of 24 April they made their way to the fishing village of Polruan. There, looking down in moonlight on to the beach, they believed they had found what they wanted.

The bay was sheltered by hills on either side, and the houses above the beach had been built on rising ground and looked down on it, tier on tier, so that the beach itself looked rather like an amphitheatre. The smaller fishing boats came in there to land their catches for a small fish market in the village. There was a miniature landing-stage, but it seemed that this was not much in use. Below the headland on which King and Cuthbertson stood lay line upon line of boats moored to stanchions. Most of them were completely above the waterline and lay on their sides on the beach, but at high tide they would all be afloat.

Polruan's streets and beach were deserted. Not a light glowed, the windows of the houses being blinded by black-out shutters. It seemed safe to descend to the beach and make a cautious scrutiny of the boats.

One of them took their fancy, a sturdy craft which they judged to be about thirty feet long. It had a mast and furled sail, but it also had an engine. They climbed up on to the stranded craft and examined it. Knowing a little about petrol-driven engines, they felt they had a good idea how it worked and found that the equipment in the boat included a tool-kit for use if necessary at sea. They wondered how far out to sea a comparatively small craft like this one could be expected to venture. On the other hand they were optimistic that it might not be too large for them to handle. It would, they decided, fit their requirements handsomely. They praised it excitedly but did not give voice to a few stray thoughts as to whether the little vessel required qualified and experienced seamen to sail her with any degree of safety.

They climbed down from her, making as little noise as possible, and moved furtively back across the beach and up again on to the cliff-top. Sometimes, as on this occasion, they were aware of a sense of acting like criminals, but always they quashed this with a conviction that it was all in rather a splendid cause. Their furtive existence made it seem that already, even before leaving England, they were judging everybody but themselves as 'the enemy', a state of mind that might have its use if they came to be hiding-out in France.

Back in the cave, they planned their get-away from Polruan beach: they would steal down into the cove after dusk, take the boat, sail her round to their own cove, load up with their gear and, setting a course which they hoped would be accurate, move out in the darkness for France. They checked the approximate times of high tide, as they would have to take the craft both at night and at a time when the one they had selected was still afloat.

This, they told each other, was to be their last night in the cave. There were no more preparations to be made. All was ready.

They settled down for a good night's rest, but they found sleep difficult. Now that the start of their adventure was imminent, they were greatly excited, and they could not prevent thoughts of possible dangers crowding their minds.

'Wonder what the trip across the Channel will be like,' remarked Cuthbertson.

'It won't be a piece of cake, that's for sure,' declared King. 'No use pretending to ourselves.'

'That's what I thought, Peter. I've never sailed a boat like that.'

'I haven't either.'

'Daresay it can be pretty rough in mid-Channel, and it's a fair way across from here.'

'Don't worry, Leslie. Leave it to your Uncle Peter. I know I was unfortunate in not getting into the commandos, but I've got the devil's own luck really. Always have.'

'D'you think we'll need it?' Cuthbertson was fully committed to the adventure, but he was not too young to know the perils that faced them – and to be concerned about them.

'We'll need all the luck in Old Nick's cupboard, Leslie. No doubt about that. The letter we've written to old Winnie – I mean Winston Churchill, mustn't be disrespectful at a time like this – has some fine phrases in it. But as sure as my name's Peter King, the Army will think we're mad.'

'But they'll think well of us.'

'Perhaps being near the start-off is giving me the jitters, Leslie, but you never can tell which way the wind blows with the Army. We've put our fingers to our nose at them, and they won't like it. What we've got to do now is to make a bloody good job of our operation.'

'Aye, that we have,' breathed Cuthbertson.

King changed the conversation. 'Tell you what, I'm bloody hungry.'

'So am I. But I'd rather starve tonight than eat any of that raw muck.'

Later they were still awake. The older man said: 'I'm all too aware what a damned risky business this is. Getting across the Channel will only be for starters. I think before we set off we should put the dangers into words. We've both got to realise what we're doing. I do, and I want to make sure you do as well.'

'You know damn well that I know what we're doing, Peter.'

'All the same, let's put it into words. We could be shot attempting to land. If we're not, we could be shot out of hand afterwards on the orders of some enthusiastic thug of a Nazi officer.'

'Or we could become prisoners of war for a hell of a long time.'

'That too.'

'You realise we'll have no papers to show. We haven't even got our AB64s, They're in the envelope to old Winnie. They might think we're spies.'

'We *will* be in uniform,' Cuthbertson reminded him.

'That's true. But if we're caught, don't you think our story would sound a bit daft? Too good to be true? Couldn't blame 'em if they thought there was something more to it than we were saying. They'd never imagine for a moment that a couple of *their* soldiers would set off on their own on such a crazy stunt.'

'Do you think we're crazy then?'

'I don't think we're crazy. But we've got to admit it's a bit of a crazy venture.'

'Surely you don't want to call it off then.'

'No, I don't. I think we've just got to do it, but I think we've got to realise now, tonight, just what we're going into. I'm just being the devil's advocate. I'm facing up to the fact that one or both of us might die, that's all. In my case I don't suppose it matters. If God decides I must – well, it's not as though I've any responsibilities to a wife or near relatives. I just want to make sure *you* realise.'

'I realise. And I'm not married either. We can't pull out now. We're going, aren't we?'

'Yes,' said King, 'we are.'

There did not seem much more to do. The sooner they made the attempt the better. They fixed the date. The next night, they decided, 'Operation Wild Dog' would really begin.

They were nevertheless relieved when morning came and

they set off to walk into Fowey. This was necessary because there was one important thing still to be done – to post the envelope containing the letter to the Prime Minister. They thrust it, together with the letter Cuthbertson had written to his mother, into the first pillar-box they came to and immediately returned to the cave to lie low for the rest of the day. The final seal had been put on their attempt. It must now go forward, they told themselves, whether they liked it or not.

When dusk fell, they set off for Polruan and settled down in the shadows of the cliff-top for the village to quieten down. It was a rather still night, with the moon sailing in and out of clouds and from time to time shedding a pale light on the beach where the boats lay. On a night like that sounds would carry far, and it was essential for the village to have closed its doors before they ventured down.

A few figures moved about on the beach. Occasional echoes of footfalls came to them from the direction of the streets. There was still some time before the tide went right out, but time was passing, and the line of surf on the shore was receding. They must reach the boat before it became beached.

When there was no sign of movement below, they began to move down – but they had to pause and wait, for there were spasmodic glows of light from a doorway on the front, followed by the sound of footsteps. They realised that it was a pub, its windows blacked out but showing a gleam every time its door opened. It was obvious that from time to time people were leaving and going home. It came as a shock to them to realise that they must wait on the cliff-top until the pub closed its doors for the night and everyone had gone home. Would they be in time to reach the boat while it still floated?

Far below, the door opened again. This time more than one came out. Their figures could be seen dimly against a moonlit backcloth. They stood talking for a few minutes before going home, and snatches of laughter echoed up to the two soldiers. How many more men were still in the pub? why didn't they all go home and leave the place conveniently deserted?

King and Cuthbertson asked themselves what the clientele of the pub were talking about. The war? The fear, not yet ruled out, of an invasion of Britain by the Germans? Or when the Allies would invade France? Everyone was anxious for that. And for that big decision by the government and the High Command *they* at least were not waiting.

Never was the slow desertion of a pub at closing-time more exasperating to two men waiting for that to happen. They had to wait for a much longer time than they had anticipated. And when they hurried at last down to the water's edge, they found the boat lying in shallow water. Already her keel was resting on the sand and pebbles. They waded in, put their hands to the boat and began to push. She did not move.

They fancied that every sound they made, as they splashed in the water and exhorted each other to more determined effort, could be heard for miles. They were in a state of anxiety and sharp disappointment. They put their shoulders to the side of the craft, but it would not budge.

When they gave up, they moved further up the beach and lay down exhausted, their caution momentarily at an end, not caring if they were discovered. Then, wet and cold, they made their way along the headland to the cave, where they squeezed out their wet uniforms and laid them out to dry. For the first time since they had set off from Aldershot, they suffered not only acute disappointment but for a time a sense of failure.

Until then, it had appeared that luck was on their side. It had been quite extraordinary luck, but was it now running out?

The excitement of their abortive attempt to commandeer a boat being over, they recalled that the letter to the Prime Minister, having been posted, was irretrievable. Within a few days Mr Churchill, the War Cabinet and the War Office would be aware of their absence from their unit and of their remarkable intentions. They were forced to realise that their getting clear of Britain was now problematical, and the search for them would no doubt be greatly intensified. It was not a comforting thought.

9 — Waiting for H-hour

The hopeful invaders fell back on their original plan of trying to hire a boat from the friendly skipper of a ferry-boat which plied round the coast to nearby resorts. In a bid to gain the man's confidence, they travelled on his craft several times, paying their fare and engaging him in conversation whenever possible.

They told the ferryman they had just completed a long and arduous tour of duty and had been granted a fairly long furlough, which they would not be surprised to find was preparatory to their being sent to a theatre of active war abroad. If only they could hire a boat to do some fishing, a sport of which they were inordinately fond, before their probable movement overseas prevented their indulging in it for 'a very long time to come'! This manner of gaining the ferryman's sympathy was not a little dangerous, as it suggested a large movement of troops – the security system in Britain was vigilant and well organised, but it was officially recognised that there was no sense in careless talk reaching the ears of enemy agents who might have managed to infiltrate into the country; posters everywhere proclaimed the warning, 'Walls Have Ears'. But the ferryman had said he knew where he might lay his hands on a boat; and the eager adventurers, aware that the letter to the Prime Minister had sped north and would soon be carried south again to London, were at urgent pains to hire that boat, one way or another.

The seaman, however, did not appear to weaken much from his claim that no unauthorised person was supposed to take a boat out. Everyone living on the coast was aware of it, he said, and of the two-mile limit order. It depended on what 'unauthorised' meant, they argued. Obviously one could not have civilians sailing about in boats in the Channel, but they were responsible soldiers – and sergeants at that. If only they could have one fishing trip before they returned to duty . . .

But two days passed without their extracting a promise from the ferryman, and they ceased taking trips on his boat, which sailed during the hours of daylight. If the postmaster in Edinburgh had despatched the envelope without waiting two days as they had requested, Mr Churchill might be reading their letter already. Consequently that could cause orders to be sent to coastal areas for special vigilance to be kept concerning two missing soldiers.

The amateur commandos were forced to view their self-appointed mission in a less optimistic frame of mind. Having come thus far towards turning their incredible dream into reality, it would be a bitter disappointment for their private invasion to end before it had begun – and at the place from which they hoped to sail. They were tempted to believe for the first time that their scheme had perhaps been too ambitious. Already for some time reason and common sense had caused them to realise that perhaps they were crazy to attempt it. That sense now became more real.

If at this stage the authorities foiled the attempt, what would happen to them? They would suffer an ignominious return to their unit, punishment, even maybe derision, for who would believe that they had really planned to execute alone a daring if incredible assault on the enemy? Their story might well be regarded as an imaginative excuse for their being absent from duty.

They agreed they could not sit waiting for that to happen and decided to have one more attempt to persuade the seaman. Knowing where he lived, they determined to risk a talk with him at his home.

They called in the early evening upon the seaman, who welcomed them into the house and asked his wife to produce a pot of tea, which was brought to them in the sitting-room, with a plate of sandwiches and some home-baked cake. For the visitors it was a feast indeed. Their optimism returned to a point where they again felt fit for anything they might be called upon to do – except return to Aldershot in the charge of military police.

As the three talked, the adventurers began to see a

glimmer of hope; their host's refusal to help them appeared to be relaxing. He could certainly lend them fishing-rods. Come to that, he knew where he could acquire some spare tins of petrol, though that was something to keep very quiet about, wartime fuel rationing being so strict.

The soldiers hinted that they would pay extremely well for hire of a boat – and many times the value of any extra petrol he got for them. They hoped to spend at least two whole days fishing.

The ferryman agreed to 'think about it' but warned them that he had not yet made any promises. Insisting that they must return his hospitality, they arranged to meet him in a local pub the following night in order to buy him a drink.

Pinning their hopes on what a pint or two of beer might accomplish, they set out the next night with high hopes. Inside the pub they felt distinctly uneasy, thinking that all eyes were upon them and that they might be challenged at any moment. Both were non-drinkers, and the few half-pints they swallowed while buying pints for their friend had an unpleasant effect on their stomachs, which, in addition to being unused to alcohol, were lacking good food.

Afterwards, as the three left the pub together, the hopeful 'commandos' were delighted and excited to be told by the seaman: 'I'll have the boat ready. Come down to the beach at midday tomorrow – and for the Lord's sake don't get me into trouble.'

The morning dawned bright and clear, with a light breeze and from their little cove the sea looked calm enough even for amateur sailors like themselves to brave.

It was 29 April. Four days had passed since they had posted their letter to the Prime Minister.

They felt much as they had on the morning, which seemed a long time ago, when they had waited for the time to set off from the barracks at Aldershot. On that occasion they had been anxious that discovery of the missing weapons might prevent their setting off. This time they feared that a coast-watch might be set up specially for them. They were extremely nervous about their chances of getting away successfully.

They spent the morning moving all their gear from the

cave to a hollow under a huge boulder which lay in the foreground of the cove. This would be much nearer the spot where they aimed to come in with the boat to load up. It would also serve as a landmark, as they had not previously approached the cove from the sea. As they would be embarking in daylight, they had no wish to arrive at the boat with packs and haversacks containing pistols, ammunition, grenades and a compass.

They also set about ridding themselves of unwanted items, as they had before leaving their unit. These included any personal letters they had received (which bore their names and might identify them), the remainder of their stolen leave-passes and rail-warrants and a few banknotes which they judged would be left over from their original £30 capital apart from that with which they would pay the ferryman. They had formed an idea that anything that might be of interest to the enemy should be left behind, and they emptied their pockets in front of each other so that both would be confident that nothing 'incriminating' had been overlooked. This time they did not burn the items but instead wrapped them in a waterproof map-case, which they placed in a respirator haversack and buried, marking the spot with a number of stones.

At midday they marched down to the waterfront at Fowey, and the ferryman, who was sitting there, took them to where the boat they were to hire was moored.

They were delighted with the craft. She was an open boat and did not appear to them to be large enough for a sea-going vessel, or capable of any great speed, and few would have contemplated using her for the type of assault they had in mind, but at least she was in reasonable condition, and they were not in a position to acquire anything better. To them she was a boat, and their only means of embarking on their adventure. From prow to stern she measured about thirty feet; she was painted blue, and her name, *Sea Bird*, had faded and was barely discernible. She was steered by a stern tiller and had an engine under a hatch forward and a mast. In the stern lay a folded, weathered, white sail, four oars and two fishing-rods.

Their friend told them that the tank was filled with

petrol, that there were two spare tins of fuel and they would find oilskins in the hatch. Before leaving them, he advised them not to go out much further than the bay itself, where, he assured them, they would get some good fishing. He also reminded them of the two-mile limit, saying that if they attempted to go further out, they would probably be loud-hailed from the coast-station at the end of the bay and, if they persisted, would probably get a warning shot across their bows.

They cast off, started the engine and cruised out into the bay, where they cut the engine, hove-to and began to make a show of fishing. Holding their rods over the side, their hooks not even baited, the exercise provided them with no relaxation as they waited impatiently for dusk, when they hoped to edge over the two-mile limit and make a dash for it. From time to time they moved a little further out, stopping each time as though trying for bites in different positions. As the afternoon wore on, they gradually edged round the headland on which stood the look-out station, hugging the land.

It was necessary to visit the cove and load up during daylight, as in darkness they might never find the stone marking their hidden kit. Keeping well inland, they made slowly for the cove. But when they lay off it, they discovered to their dismay that they were still in view of the coast-station, which was at the nearer end of the boom. Their every move loading up must surely be perceived. Not having checked on this did not accord with their usual care and caution, but it revealed that they possessed the human capacity for error.

They slackened speed and cruised round in a tight little circle, wondering how best they could take on their gear without causing suspicion. They looked at the squat, fortress-like station, its windows flashing in the sunlight, and then turned their gaze to the deserted cove and the isolated stone under which lay their invasion material. The station could not be seen from the cave, nor the cave from the station, but the place they had left their gear could. Perhaps men at the station had watched them hiding it. Possibly it would be from that station that the two petty-officers to whom they had chatted had started their patrol.

The last week had been the most anxious time for them since they left Aldershot. But there was danger in looking back, and they must think forward. Above all other considerations they had acquired a boat, and that at one time had seemed impossible.

The decision what to do was, they believed, made for them, rather than making it. They must go in and put the stuff aboard. There was nothing else for it. They must just risk it.

For about half an hour they hove-to, pretending to fish from the same spot, placing their reliance on the hope that those who manned the station might expect them to remain there and would relax their watch for a time.

King, who was at the tiller, then ordered Cuthbertson to speed up the engine, and they chugged in slowly towards the beach. Having learned a lesson with the boat they could not get seaborne at Polruan, they were careful not to run their craft too far in, leaving it, by means of its small anchor, in a few feet of water.

They passed back and forward as quickly as they could between the rock and the boat, carrying their material. All thought of pretending to picnic in the cove or appearing innocently unhurried was cast aside. They just did the job as speedily as possible, expecting every moment to be hailed.

At last all was aboard, and they re-started the engine and moved out, repressing a desire to make straight out to sea at full speed. Some distance out, they hove-to and pretended once more to fish, as though nothing unusual had happened at the cove.

Eventually a measure of confidence returned. They looked round the boat, taking stock of their material assets. There were their packs and haversacks containing revolvers, ammunition, grenades, tins of black boot-polish, compass, towels, soap, wire-cutters and pliers. Tied to their packs were their waterproof groundsheet capes. A bag contained a large chunk of stale bread (they had bought a loaf several days before and eaten half of it) and half a dozen apples (similarly acquired). A two-gallon can was full of drinking-water, and there were two army water-bottles, also filled with water. The boat had a full tank of petrol, and there was extra fuel in their own and those tins provided by the ferryman, amounting in all, they judged, to about 27 gallons.

They were rather proud of the equipment they had acquired, but they were not yet on their way to France, and they were still far from sanguine about that possibility. They still had the two-mile limit to cross, and they were aware that that would be the greatest test yet of the manner in which fortune was prepared to favour them. They were plagued by uneasy thoughts as to whether orders had reached Cornwall for a look-out to be kept for the 'escaping' British soldiers. Earlier they had hidden their battledress uniforms by putting on the oilskins left in the boat for them by their ferryman friend, but a number of people, including no doubt men at the coastguard station, had seen them step into the boat and push off wearing uniform.

They would have felt infinitely better if they could have set out to brave the Channel as soon as they cast off at Fowey. Too much time still remained until dusk, when they would be expected to come in from their fishing expedition, and their nervous fears and imaginings gave them several unpleasant hours. They were prey to all kinds of thoughts – that the British Navy would be sweeping the waters they aimed to cross, ready to intercept them at any moment, maybe looking for them; nearer to France German craft might be patrolling the French waters; and there was the sea itself, miles and miles of deepness and darkness and, for all they knew, a great deal of wind to blow untrained and inexperienced sailors completely off course.

They were at last humbled into the realisation that the private contribution they hoped to make to the war effort did not bear further contemplating – only, God willing, attempting.

10 — Strange Letter for No. 10

On that same day, 29 April, the letter which Cuthbertson and King had posted to the Prime Minister was delivered to his official address in London, No. 10 Downing Street, and intelligence officers were puzzling over its remarkable contents. For the first time, eighteen days after the would-be invaders had left their unit, the authorities had a sign that something unusual might be taking place.

The letter was at once handed over to Major Desmond Morton, CMG, MC, Mr Churchill's personal adviser on intelligence. Studying it closely, together with the enclosed Army Pay Books, he did not know what to make of it. On the face of it, two soldiers of the Dental Corps, presumably untrained and inexperienced in such military action, were giving notice that they were attempting, without any sort of permission, and certainly not as part of an official military operation, an outrageous and surely impossible task. It did not seem feasible. Was it, then, a practical joke? Was the letter not in fact written by these two soldiers? Had some army jester gained possession of comrades' pay-books and sent the letter in their name? Many thoughts occurred to suggest that no such private assault on the coast of France was about to take place.

Major Morton sought the reaction of other officers to the information the letter contained. They noted that it had been posted in Edinburgh. Why Edinburgh? To that there was no answer, and probably would not be when the postal authorities in that city were contacted. As it transpired, the Post Office officials in the Scottish capital had obeyed the instructions in the covering letter, waiting for two days before forwarding it – it was not unknown for the Post Office to receive strange requests during wartime. That the covering letter was also signed by King did not necessarily mean that he had written it. The envelope containing the one for the Prime Minister had, according to the staff of the postmaster in Edinburgh, been mislaid or destroyed, and the postmark, indicating where it had been posted originally, was therefore unknown. Another stroke of luck for King and Cuthbertson!

The conference Major Morton held with fellow intelligence officers came to no conclusion, though a number of interesting theories were put forward and either noted or dismissed. Some of those present favoured the theory that it was the work of some crackpot. It was hardly likely that an enemy agent or Nazi sympathiser had sent the message, since an attempt to mislead the British authorities over a small, ineffectual and no doubt bogus raid would cause little embarrassment. On the other hand, could this be part of a clever plot to get two German agents *into* the country?

At this stage the letter gave rise to a number of fascinating ideas, and for the time being nothing was ruled out.

It was imperative that the matter be thoroughly investigated, and if this pointed to the authors of the remarkable letter being completely truthful in what they had written, if they indeed contemplated such a raid and intended to attempt it, then it would be not only an astonishing plan but also highly irregular.

The opinion of the meeting was that even a body of trained men from a commando unit would consider such an attempt useless unless it were planned at a high level. Not even they, let alone a couple of Dental Corps chaps, would consider going off half-cock, as it were, and without permission, on such a dangerous mission.

All were agreed that if by some wide stretch of the imagination the escapade outlined in the letter were *bona fide*, the two men concerned could be properly described as desperadoes or crazy fools.

One of the first moves to make, Major Morton decided, would be to check on whether the two soldiers named on the pay-books were in fact absent from their units, either with or without leave. It was also decided to contact the Special Operations Executive, which controlled British agents in Occupied France and was responsible for getting them into the country. This was normally effected by dropping them as parachutists from aircraft, and if some other means of transport were about to be tried out, Major Morton was ignorant of it. The SOE, however, was one of the more unusual departments – could they be using these two soldiers in some manner important to them? Had they ever heard of the two men? It was well worth a check.

If the letter were in fact a truthful account of the men's intentions, then, according to its contents and the date of the postmark, they would have attempted to leave the country three days previously. And no reports had been made of anyone's trying to do so.

No action was taken that day.

Meanwhile King and Cuthbertson sat in their boat drifting at a position they judged to be a little inside the two-mile limit.

Two factors promoted a state of excitement: they were afloat and all ready to go – but for a time yet they must contain their enthusiasm. Thoughts of the letter they had sent to Downing Street prompted fears that the coastguard service might have been alerted already to watch for a suspicious move such as they were making, and whether this had occurred or not, it was the duty of the coast-watch to bring in any straying craft before dusk should fall.

All conversation in the boat ended. They could think of nothing to say. They ceased all pretence of fishing.

They had stopped asking each other why they had not been challenged following their loading-up operation from the cove, which could easily have been seen by the shore-station, and congratulating themselves that the remarkable luck they had had so far was still operating in their favour. But they remained distinctly ill at ease.

Towards evening the breeze moderated, and as the sun began to go down, a strange calm seemed to envelop them. The sense of stillness was heightened because their engine had been cut off. No other craft was in sight, the coastline and the sea horizon were becoming less distinct, and the diminishing swell produced less slapping on the sides of the boat. They wondered for a time if they had drifted further from land and were probably a little beyond the two-mile limit. On the other hand, they reassured themselves, the haze that lay over land and sea was no doubt due to the slow coming of the dusk. But eventually they became aware that this was due also to something else – the slow materialisation of a sea-mist. This grew thicker. Soon the coastline was blotted out, and out to sea the horizon vanished.

For the two, amateur sailors that they were, it was more than a little alarming. They were at the mercy of the compass, which they had set approximately for Cherbourg. But they were also aware that nothing could have suited their purpose better than the onset of the sea-mist. They could not see the land, but neither could they be seen by the coastguard. They lost no time in starting the engine and moving rapidly away from England. For a time they were elated, slapping each other on the back and singing snatches of song.

The exhilaration brought about by what they described as their 'getaway', did not, however, last long. New concerns and imaginary fears took its place. Had they set the compass correctly? They knew how to use such an instrument on land, but was there, they asked each other, a slightly different way of using it at sea? Did they have to make allowances for influences which did not apply on land? They realised just how amateur they were as seamen. On the wastes of water it was not difficult to imagine that they might be so off-course that they could sail for hours and never reach France. Worse still, in the grey eddies of the mist they could run into some other craft. Eventually they ceased voicing their fears. In the position in which they now found themselves, firmly launched on their voyage to France, it would not have improved matters.

The thing they understood a little better than the compass, however, was the engine – and that was behaving beautifully, droning on sweetly and healthily.

As they chugged on, settling down to a long night's sail, excitement was replaced by hunger, and from their meagre food stock each ate some dry bread and munched an apple.

They might have added a few knots to their speed if they had run up a sail, but this they dared not do, fearing that with their lack of experience and skill the boat might become unbalanced. And as events were to prove, the decision was a wise one.

As darkness closed in around them, the mist began to disperse, or they ran out of it. For a time the blackness was preferable to the walls of greyness, for they believed they would more easily discern the lights or shapes of other craft. They fully expected to see and hear other human life, as the Channel must be well patrolled by naval vessels and no doubt also by aircraft. But with the clearer weather came rougher seas, choppy at first, then heaving with big, rolling waves.

It began to rain, and a bitter wind lashed it into their faces and flung spray high over their prow. They rummaged for the oilskins the ferryman had provided, which they had worn while fishing, and put them on again; these helped to counter the wind, but they were miserably cold; their army greatcoats, which they had been unable to bring as well as the other equipment, would have been greatly welcomed as additional protection.

They felt, so far, that the worsening weather might be described as a squall, and if that were the case they should survive it, despite its unpleasantness.

But they had a long way to go, and there was no way of knowing if it would get rougher. Making as they were from Cornwall to the Cherbourg area, they had some 130 miles of open sea to negotiate, more if they failed to keep precisely on course or if they were blown off it. It was one of the widest parts of the Channel to cross (Portsmouth to Le Havre could be about 100 miles, Brighton to Dieppe still less, and Hastings to Boulogne a matter of 50 miles), but they had reckoned that getting away from Britain any further east of Cornwall would have been more difficult because of the presence of larger towns and military concentrations. Similarly, they estimated that trying to land east of the Cherbourg peninsula would be more dangerous – a theory that still had to be tested.

As they sailed on, the wind grew stronger and the swell increased. The *Sea Bird* began to pitch more alarmingly. It seemed probable that the squall was developing into a gale. What drills of seamanship must then be put into effect for a boat of that size? King had an idea that in that event they should steer straight into the gale. But precisely how that should be accomplished both were completely ignorant, and it seemed that a craft as small as theirs would be entirely at the mercy of the elements.

The boat began to roll as well as pitch. The wind blew harder; the waves grew larger still, and heavier rain was hurled at them. When the *Sea Bird* breasted the waves, it slewed deeper than ever into the troughs. To the two hopefuls the sea seemed largely composed of mountains and valleys. Eventually they found it almost impossible to steer.

One of the 'luxuries' with which they had to do without during their amateur attack was the provision of a detailed weather forecast for this stretch of water and the French coastal area. An officially mounted raid would not only have had this benefit, it would no doubt have taken the forecast into consideration in order to choose the moment of departure from England.

Before midnight, and with the conditions deteriorating all the time, Cuthbertson became seasick. King ordered him to rest as best he could, himself hanging on to the tiller and struggling. But within a quarter of an hour King was also vomiting, while Cuthbertson crawled aft to help him with the tiller. Together they sprawled, both hanging on to it, both vomiting.

They were still sick when they realised that cold water was lapping and rising at their ankles. The boat was becoming waterlogged due both to shipping water from the big waves and to the heavy rain. Strenuously they began baling out the water, using their caps and then an empty petrol-can and a saucepan with no handle which they found in a hatch forward. From time to time as they baled they still vomited.

Some time after midnight the gale abated, and after a time the sickness left them, but they were more fatigued than at any time since their training began or since they had left Aldershot. When the remains of the water were baled out, they began to take an interest again in sighting any other craft that might come upon them. While one took charge of the boat, the other kept a lookout for the approach of any such vessel. But through the rest of that long night, during which wind and sea calmed and visibility became reasonable, they spotted neither a gleam of light nor the shape of any ship. At times they must have been fairly close to either a Royal Navy patrol-ship or a mine-sweeper, but not one was ever near enough to see or be seen. Not once did an aircraft pass over in their vicinity.

Dawn came with a pale glow in the east and as the sky became lighter, the sea was still empty except for their own little boat. And nothing came within view as hour after hour they headed steadily for France.

Thankful to have survived the gale, shivering, uncomfortable and not so far having quite recovered from their bouts of sickness, their optimism was nevertheless a little damaged. Each admitted, privately, that they might not reach France (there was still no landfall), and long silences developing between them indicated that the gale and their physical miseries had dampened their enthusiasm, albeit only at the edges.

King broke the long silence to say that it was imperative that they land in France and try to create some damage. If they were prevented in any way from doing so, and still managed to return to England, they could be treated, at worst, he believed, as traitors who had been trying to join the enemy. At best they could be ridiculed. Cuthbertson reminded his companion that their letter to the Prime Minister, with their army pay-books as proof of identity, would be looked upon as good intention. King replied wryly that it was difficult to beat the official mind if it were intent on punishment.

Apart from all considerations of escaping official wrath, however, it was quite impossible, having come thus far, to turn back. Nor did they really wish to. It was just that a little sound thought was balancing their quixoticism.

One of them even voiced the suggestion that the manner in which they had slunk out of Britain was more consistent with their being criminals or spies than patriotic soldiers determined to get into action against the enemy. He said so jokingly, adding that he hoped the authorities would not come to look on their action in this light.

As the morning passed, the sky became blue and cloudless and the sea reasonably calm. They spoke of the sickness they had suffered during the night and wondered if it had been caused by their recent raw and unsatisfactory diet as much as by the violence of the gale. By midday, with the sun bright and warm, their spirits rose, and their enterprise was again characterised by optimism.

When they made landfall, it wanted several hours to dusk. Cuthbertson, who was in the prow, pointed and shouted for his comrade to look ahead. On the horizon there was a thin dark line, and a few minutes later there was no doubt that this was a coastline. They could not, of course, go in during daylight. They switched off the engine and allowed the boat to drift.

Cuthbertson thought that the coastline ahead looked suspiciously like the one that had been swallowed in the mist the previous evening, but he did not say so. A similar thought came to King, and he voiced it. 'I hope it *is* France,' he said.

'If it's not France, then it could only be one of the Channel Isles,' said Cuthbertson, reluctant to give credence to his first disconcerting impression.

King said he believed it could not be the Channel Isles, otherwise they would have reached them sooner, because they had kept going all night, and their route, according to their compass setting, should have by-passed them.

'It *must* be France,' said his companion. King agreed, and they laughed, clapped each other on the back and even shook hands as though to seal a bargain.

But they had a long time to remain inactive before darkness came, and as time passed, they became uneasy again. Every time they looked landwards, they saw the coastline more like that of England. Could they have made a terrible navigational error? After all, they were amateur seamen. And what the gale might have done was to them a matter of question. Could their little compass have gone wrong? Could they in some way have turned in a full circle back towards England?

‘Impossible!’ they agreed, but not very convincingly.

There was only one way to find out, and that entailed sweating it out until nightfall and then doing so in a particularly dangerous manner. Even if they got ashore without being spotted, it would be a very simple matter to meet a German patrol within a very short time of doing so. It was best to try not to think about such possibilities. A more urgent fear was that in the hours of daylight that remained they might be spotted before they even tried to move in. There must surely be German seacraft, and perhaps aircraft, so near to Occupied France. Tension was high for them as they spent hours straining eyes and ears.

When they had caught their first glimpse of the coast their wristwatches had shown the time as 7 p.m. They had been in the boat for thirty-two hours, and the actual voyage from dusk of the previous day had taken some twenty-two hours.

11 — Point of No Return

They settled down to wait for darkness to fall. It would be several hours before even the dusk came, and there was nothing they could do but remain completely inactive.

The day remained bright, and visibility was good – too good for their purpose. They were drifting at what they thought might be two or more miles from land and could see the coastline plainly. But they must surely be clearly visible from the shore, specially through binoculars or telescopes.

After a time they decided to move further away from the coast and, not knowing how far the noise of their engine would carry, and fearing that to move by its power would seem less like drifting, they used the oars with which the boat had been provided. This gave them something to do and had the effect to some extent of quelling their apprehensions and calming their nerves. They pulled at the oars for perhaps an hour and then allowed the craft to drift again. The land had disappeared behind them, but they had no idea what distance they had covered, a mile perhaps, they thought.

They checked the time by their watches more often than was necessary as it was still light and they could see far into the distance – so far that Cuthbertson, shading his eyes against the sun, saw a dark speck in the sky over towards where the coast lay. He kept his eyes on it, and it appeared to be growing a little larger. Then they heard a faint drone, which seemed to click on and off again. Eventually there was no doubt what it was. A plane.

The obvious fear was that they had been spotted when they had lain two miles off-shore before rowing further out. A number of disquieting possibilities presented themselves to them: that a reconnaissance plane might have been alerted to investigate their boat; that German aircraft might patrol the coast area several times a day.

The sound of the aircraft became a steady drone, growing louder, and it became obvious that it would pass right over them. Soon they could see the shape of it, but they were unable to identify it as to type or nationality. It was disheartening to realise that they might be inviting enemy interest at this time, specially after a voyage during which they had seen no sign of life and when an attempted landing appeared to be almost within their grasp. It was a situation in which they were quite helpless. Several miles out from land, there was no way in which the boat could be concealed. Inevitably she must be seen.

It was unlikely, however, that the plane was as yet near enough to have spotted two figures sitting on a seat amidships, and the idea came to them that there was perhaps one thing they could do to lessen the danger. They could try to conceal themselves in the hope that the aircraft might think it an empty boat. At once they set about doing this. King, the smaller man, managed to squeeze into the small hatch forward, and Cuthbertson lay in the bottom of the boat at the after end, covering himself completely with both oilskin coats.

They remained in hiding while the noise of the plane grew louder. By the sound of it, the aircraft appeared to pass right above them, but at what height they had no means of knowing. It did not, so far as they could make out, return and circle over them, but in case it was not far away and would return for a closer look, they stayed where they were for quite a long time, and when they at last showed themselves, there was nothing to be heard except the sound of the sea and the cries of gulls. There was no sign of the plane.

Had it, they asked, returned to report a small, unmanned boat drifting in the sea? Was it a routine flight, and had the crew, seeing what appeared to be an empty boat, taken little interest and flown on? But they found it impossible to discount what remained their worst fear – that the crew of the plane might have noted something suspicious about the boat and its contents and returned to land to report the matter, and that soon a German vessel would be on its way to investigate the *Sea Bird* more closely. All the questions they asked about the appearance of the plane, however, had to remain matters of conjecture, and, as on other occasions since the escapade began, they had to trust to luck. Again they waited for the dark.

With the coming of twilight they began their preparations for an attempted landing. From their haversacks they took their tins of bootpolish and blackened their faces and hands. They checked and loaded their revolvers, put on the safety-catches, buckled on their web belts and placed their weapons securely in the attached holsters. They put on their packs and haversacks, filling them with their wire-cutters and pliers, the remainder of their gear and the rest of the ammunition and grenades, which they divided between them. Their commando knives they fixed to their belts. Then they drank from their water-bottles, refilled them from the can of drinking water they had brought and slung them over their shoulders. Their remaining stock of food – a little bread and four apples – they stuffed into their pockets.

They were in battle-dress tunic and trousers, boots and short web gaiters. On their heads they wore forage-caps. (Steel helmets, they had decided earlier, would have been suspicious items with which to have been seen going on leave.)

When it was completely dark, they started the engine and, keeping it throttled back, cruised slowly towards the coast. Eventually they silenced the engine and began cautiously rowing the last mile.

It was 11 p.m. On the land ahead they could make out a few dimmed lights but no sign or sound of movement. They steered away from that area and pointed their prow towards a darker land-mass which had no lights – or lights perhaps better masked.

Completely without incident they came in under a high, dark cliff, thankful that the sea was not rough and that they were not dashed on to the rocks. The boat scraped against a rocky ledge, and they grabbed at it to prevent the craft's floating off again. For several minutes they remained there, listening anxiously for any sound that might indicate that their arrival had been observed. They were gratified, though surprised, to find that there were no such sounds and no sign of life. As their eyes became more accustomed to the darkness below the cliff, they became aware that a little further along there was a small inlet, which they made for, taking pains not to splash with the oars. Gaining their objective, they secured the boat, and with a few uprooted wild plants and weeds, but mostly with seaweed, they made an attempt to camouflage it. This was not altogether successful, but as the craft lay inside the inlet and under overhanging cliffs, it was unlikely that it would be spotted either from above or from the sea, and might remain undiscovered for some time unless a special search were made.

Scaling the high cliffs would present a difficult if not dangerous task, but to have rowed further along the coast looking for a place easier of access would no doubt have invited discovery. As it was, they were only too pleased to have come to land without, so far as they were aware, having been seen.

They had practised climbing cliffs in Cornwall, and this one did not appear to be beyond their capabilities, though they had failed to bring with them the rope which they had used on those earlier ascents. Slowly they began to worm their way upwards, helping each other as best they could and trying to take their time despite their excitement. Several times their feet slipped and slid downwards, but they dared not speak and held their breath because of the noise this made – a noise intensified by their state of mind. On one occasion Cuthbertson, who was climbing behind King, broke the descent of his comrade: fortunately his feet had a firm hold on a rock, and he also managed to hold on firmly, both hands digging deeply into grass roots. It was a dangerous moment, as both men might have been hurled to the bottom of the cliff.

They were by that time committed to continuing the climb, for to try to make their way down again would have been even more dangerous. After a few minutes' rest they continued upwards, losing their footing again several times but luckily not sliding far back.

The ascent, made in darkness and with no sound except the sea-wind and the noise of the waves on the rocks below, was not a little frightening. But their main fear was what and whom they would encounter when they reached the cliff-top.

12 — Puzzle for the War Office

On the morning of 30 April, some twelve hours before the amateur commandos began to scale the cliff on the French coast, Major Morton, still puzzling over the strange letter which had arrived for Mr Churchill some twenty-four hours previously, began to take action.

In his office in London a copy of the letter was made, and he ordered that the original, together with the pay-books, be sent to Miss C. M. Campbell, private secretary to the Secretary of State for War, at the War Office. The wording of the covering letter, written by one of his assistants, F. D. W. Brown, and marked 'SECRET', was:

> 30 April 1942
>
> URGENT
>
> Dear Miss Campbell,
>
> I enclose a copy of a letter from a Sergeant King of the Army Dental Corps. The whole thing may of course be a hoax. Nevertheless steps are being taken to inform SOE, and I should be grateful if you would let me have anything you may be able to find out discreetly from the men's unit, as to whether they have in fact been posted absent, with dates, and as to their character, etc.
>
> You should also be in possession of their pay-books, enclosed with Sergeant King's letter, and I am therefore sending them to you.
>
> Yours sincerely,
> F.D.W.B.
>
> Miss C. M. Campbell,
> War Office.

Brown put a handwritten note at the top of the letter: 'Major Morton has a copy and will inform SOE.'

Everyone in Major Morton's department who read the letter signed by King was of the opinion not only that it presented an intriguing mystery but that the writing of it to the Prime Minister was unique. If it in fact described a true intention by the two soldiers concerned, they said, then such an action would be unique too.

Major Morton also put into practice a decision he had

made earlier to contact Colonel Brien Clarke of the Special Operations Executive, which controlled British agents in France. He despatched the following letter to the colonel, written by himself and also marked 'SECRET'.

30 April 1942

SECRET

Dear Brien Clarke,

Attached please find a copy of a somewhat unusual letter addressed to the Prime Minister which, though undated, arrived yesterday, having been posted in the Edinburgh district. It was accompanied by two pay-books belonging to Sergeant King and Private Cuthbertson, who are presumably the signatory and the person named in the attached.

We have examined the pay-books. They show rather a fine record for Sergeant King as a Regular soldier. He has apparently got second-class certificate of education and is working for his first-class. He has passed a course or two with distinction and is a PT instructor. His money affairs appear to be in order. Private Cuthbertson, on the other hand, seems a very ordinary sort of bloke, and there is little to be gathered from his pay-book.

Being of a nasty suspicious nature, my first wonder was whether this business was elaborate camouflage for desertion. This is always possible. In consequence, the original letter and the pay-books have been sent to the private secretary of the Secretary of State for War, asking for inquiries to be made whether these two gentlemen have disappeared from their unit, and whether there is any fruther evidence suggesting that they may really have carried out the project described in the letter.

We shall hear in due course (Note 'in due course') from the War Office, meanwhile, in case this letter be genuine in every sense, I have thought it well to send you a copy. What you can do, you alone know, but I am sure you will at least be interested in what is a very rum go.

By the way, there is no evidence in the two pay-books of either of these men that they can speak any French. The betting would be to the contrary.

Yours ever,
D. Morton.

Colonel Brien Clarke,
64 Baker Street,
W1

Colonel Clarke immediately began his own enquiries after acknowledging Major Morton's letter in these words; written from his SOE headquarters in Baker Street,

London, which in the interests of secrecy bore the innocent description 'Inter-Services Research Bureau':

> Dear Desmond (if I may?),
>
> Thank you so much for your letter of 30 April (subject – a grand chap Sgt King and his pal Cuthbertson), and I have asked Colin Gubbins if he can find out anything further about this, as it is particularly in his field of operations, and I will let you know if we have any trace.
>
> Sgt King certainly has 'the bulge' on SOE in one respect and that is he is clearly ignorant of the fact that he ought to have consulted the FO before he contemplated any such ungentlemanly acts as those he envisages!
>
> Yours ever,
> Brien Clarke.

This letter set the tone of the manner in which the Army authorities were to consider the matter for some time to come. Opinion that the whole thing might be hoax gave way to considerations that, fantastic and ridiculous though it may seem, something of the nature of an ill-advised 'private war' was taking place, conducted without permission and in an ill-conceived manner by two high-spirited soldiers entirely on their own initiative. If so, there was little that could now be done about it until some further development occurred in connection with it. Certainly it appeared that the action of the two adventurers could not now be prevented.

Major Morton waited for the SOE to enquire into whether there was some chance that the two men were being used in some secret manner as yet unknown to either Army Intelligence or the High Command. Fears that something sinister was going on – apart from military offences being committed – were largely laid aside.

Certainly everyone who now knew about the letter agreed that it was surely the most amazing ever to have been written to a prime minister in time of war by two ordinary soldiers.

The mystery remained unsolved for some time, and if King and Cuthbertson were to accomplish nothing more, they had certainly succeeded in astounding and intriguing the authorities.

13 — The Enemy has Landed

King and Cuthbertson reached the top of the cliff, scrambled over the brink and lay flat in the darkness, listening intently. They could hear no sign of movement, and there were no sounds that could be identified as human beings, vehicles or alarm-systems of any kind.

They rose to a kneeling position and looked around. There was nothing to be seen within the range of their vision except long grass, bushes and some scattered stones before them and the gleam of the sea behind. They were greatly surprised, for they had expected a totally different state of affairs and had tuned their minds to it.

Even though they had landed without interception, they had anticipated being met on the headland with the sound of movement – warning-sirens possibly, armed men perhaps closing in on them. In the event, what they experienced was an anticlimax, and it was several minutes before they could appreciate their good fortune as they whispered to each other that the part of the coast they had chanced on was not apparently near to any look-out, military concentration, village or enemy coastal-post. If there were a periodic coast-patrol, on either land or sea, they had evidently missed it.

More than at any other time since their adventure began, they were greatly aware of the astonishing luck that appeared to attend all their efforts.

It was, however, essential to move away from such open ground and to gain some sort of cover, so they began to crawl inland on their stomachs through the long grass, a method of movement which they had practised so assiduously in England. When they had covered some distance in this fashion, they came to a hedge and on crawling through it found themselves at the side of a road. This they must cross, for they had not yet found anywhere suitable for a hiding-place. Crouching under the hedge, they looked down the road both ways. There was no moon, for which they were thankful, but nor was it a very black night, and they saw that a little to their right there was a fork in the road.

Before crossing over, they decided to move cautiously up to the fork in the hope of finding a signpost, not with any idea of following it (their intention was to avoid highways, towns and villages) but to discover for certain if they were in France and, if possible, at which part of the coast, approximately, they had made their landing.

The sign, the lettering of which they read with some difficulty in the gloom, settled one thing – that they were indeed in France. But they remained ignorant of what part of the country they were in. The two names on the sign were unmistakably those of French townships or villages, but none that they had ever heard of. Neither could speak or read French, and they soon forgot the names.

The road was a rural one, and there was no house or building anywhere in sight. Nor was there a sound of traffic, even in the distance.

King suggested they should not cross over together. He ran across first, bending low, and then, after a pause, Cuthbertson joined him. Crawling through the hedge, they continued to strike inland across open fields. Knowing they had actually landed on enemy territory and having thus far met no opposition, their apprehensions lessened a little, and their confidence increased. So they began to move on foot, bending low but pausing from time to time to lie quietly on the ground.

It was imperative that they find somewhere to 'hole up' before dawn. If they could find shelter, they could remain there during the whole of the next day, their object being to move only at night committing acts of sabotage in darkness and finding natural hiding-places in which to remain during the hours of light. As time passed, their caution was further undermined by feelings of exultation and exhilaration. The pair were nothing if not enthusiastic, and they told each other in a whispered consultation when they paused for a rest-period that they were eager to do one act of sabotage before the time came for their first day's rest.

Just supposing they were captured (they avoided using the words 'shot' or 'killed') before they had the 'chance to do *something*', as Cuthbertson put it . . .

That they had survived a gale in a small boat, made the voyage and landed successfully and apparently unobserved was accomplishment enough in little more than a day and a night. But that was now in the past, and the nature of their adventure was such that they felt they must not wait too long before getting into some sort of action. If they were dug out of a hole, so to speak, before committing one hostile act, they would not easily forgive themselves.

Eventually they came to a wider road, bounded on one side by tall posts taking wires across the country. Whether these were telephone, telegraph or electricity lines they had no means of knowing, but in the spirit of their adventure they presented an inviting proposition.

They lay at the side of the road for about a quarter of an hour, and during that time no vehicles passed. It was very quiet. King produced their wire-cutters, pointed to one of the posts and said: 'Want to be first to have a go then?'

Cuthbertson was to have the honour of being first to try to cause some inconvenience to the Germans.

If he heard the slightest noise while he was working, King said, he was to get down quickly and take cover. If King heard any suspicious noise, he would whistle a warning. Taking the tool, Cuthbertson crossed the road and climbed one of the posts. When he reached the wires, he waited for a few moments, anxiously looking up and down the highway and across the fields. Nothing was to be seen, and all was quiet. He then set to work and severed five wires. Then he climbed back down to join King, who was crouching at the foot of the pole and keeping a keen watch.

To King, waiting impatiently below and being unoccupied, his companion had seemed to be aloft for a long time.

'Good work, Les,' said the sergeant, relieved that the job had been completed and that his comrade was safely on the ground again. 'But it took you a bloody long time.'

'It takes longer than you think,' replied Cuthbertson. 'You have a go and find out.'

'I mean to,' said King. 'I must have a go myself with those cutters. But it's no use cutting the same wires in a different place.'

Cuthbertson then informed the sergeant that while he was at the top of the pole he believed he had seen a line of poles leading across the field instead of alongside it. They moved cautiously down the field and alongside the road in the direction indicated by Cuthbertson, and found that the younger man had been correct in his assumption. A line of posts led across the field at right angles with the road, carrying the wiring-system in a different direction. They chose the first pole in the field, and King prepared to scale it.

'Right then,' said Cuthbertson, good-naturedly. 'We'll have a competition to see who does the job quicker. I'll time you.'

The sergeant climbed up and set to work with the wire-cutters. He soon found that his comrade was correct: the wires were not easy to sever. With some difficulty he completed the task and descended to be informed by Cuthbertson that he had taken five minutes longer to cut the same number of wires.

As they progressed inland, both that night climbed two posts each and cut twenty wires between them, Cuthbertson being declared the winner having taken eight minutes less time in all than King. Within a few hours of their landing, and despite the obvious danger of their being alone in enemy territory, the operations of that night were taking on the atmosphere of a game, and a sense of humour was helping to lessen their natural fears.

Moving on, they concentrated on finding a place where they might lie-up during the day. They had decided to avoid using a shed, barn or other building as a shelter. It was very open terrain, with only bushes and hedges breaking the contours of the fields, and they guessed that it was an agricultural area. Dawn must break soon, and they began to wonder if they would find a 'bolt-hole' in time. Already the sky was growing paler and the landscape more discernible. But at last they saw, a little to their right, a darker mass than would be made by a single tree or bush.

They made for this landmark, trotting silently on the grass now because very soon it would be first light.

Their luck was in once more. It was a copse set among what appeared to be farm fields. Inside the group of trees they found a hollow which would be an excellent hiding-place, and they looked around for anything with which they might contruct a makeshift roof over their heads to camouflage it. They found two leafy branches which had been severed or pulled from a tree. These they placed over the declivity and crawled underneath. The bottom of the hollow was wet and soggy, but they were thankful to have found a natural hiding-place, and they had anticipated that there, as in Cornwall, they would have to put up with some discomfort.

For a short time they slept, but then cold and hunger awakened them. They examined what remained of their 'iron rations' and found they possessed a hunk of stale bread about three inches thick and four apples. They ate half the bread between them and an apple each and took a swig from their water-bottles. The energy they had spent crossing the Channel, climbing the cliff, severing what they decided must be a communication system and moving inland had not exhausted them, for they were both healthy men, and their self-imposed training had made them very fit, but it had greatly tired them, and when their hunger was partially satisfied, they fell asleep again.

By 7.30 a.m. they were again awake, shivering with the cold and the wetness of their refuge. Half an hour later they heard the rattle of a train, but they did not venture to the edge of the copse to try to find in which direction, and how far away from them, the line lay. A little later they became aware of grinding noises accompanied by the whine and burr of a motor-engine. It was in the distance but eventually became recognisable as the noise of a lorry. And it was coming towards them, nearer and nearer all the time.

For some minutes they were apprehensive, but then the sound began to recede, and soon all was quiet again. The vehicle must have passed fairly close to the copse, which meant that there was a road nearby, one which they had not seen as they arrived there during the night. Remaining in their hole, they had of course not gained a glimpse of the vehicle and were unaware whether it was being used for civilian purposes or to transport soldiers. They were left to speculate on whether it was moving men into the area in order to carry out a search of the terrain.

After a time they crawled out of the hollow and had the benefit of sitting on drier ground, though they remained in the centre of the copse. As the day warmed, their spirits rose, and their sense of boldness and curiosity increased, so they crawled to the edge of the copse and very carefully peered out.

They found that the road along which the lorry had trundled lay not far away, at the edge of the field which contained their copse. At the same side they could make out a few lonely farms in the distance. When they crawled to the other side, they saw the buildings of what appeared to be a village, which they judged might be two or three miles away on rising ground.

For the whole of that day discretion superseded valour, and they remained inside the copse. They reasoned that their activities of the previous night must have resulted in loss of communication and that a search must be in progress to discover what had caused this. The severed wires must soon be found, and the Germans would be at pains to find the persons responsible. They might suspect it was the work of patriotic Frenchmen.

The two refugees were confident that they had raised no alarm after they made their landing, but the German mind was not so unimaginative as to rule out the presence of British saboteurs. Thinking along such lines, the two remained for the rest of the day not only within the island of their trees but in their uncomfortable hole. Occasionally they whispered to each other, but for the most part they maintained a strict silence. They took it in turns to sleep, but they lay in cramped positions and were victims of a growing tension. Occasionally they dozed, and some time about midday, when some warmth from the sun found its way into the hollow, inadvertently both fell asleep.

They were awakened by a noise which, when they

became fully conscious, turned out to be disturbing. It was the barking of dogs.

Their natural apprehensions suggested to them that the enemy were employing dogs to flush them out. To have broken cover, however, would not have improved matters, and there was nothing to do but lie very still and hope for the best. Eventually they realised that not only was the barking some distance away, but the dogs appeared to be remaining in the same place. They began to hope that the animals belonged to some local farmer and that they might even be chained up.

During the afternoon they took out the remaining piece of bread but with the exercise of will-power decided to save it. They chewed grass, as they had done in Cornwall, but were unable to swallow it, and they took some more sips from their water-bottles.

It was the first day they had not shaved since they left their barracks at Aldershot. Even in the boat on the day after the gale they had managed to do so, using soap and sea-water. But there was no water in the copse, and there was no question of their using any of their precious drinking -water. They were surprised to find, for the first time in their lives, that shaving provided a sort of psychological refreshment, which on that day, in the midst of obvious danger, was sadly lacking.

Trains passed at intervals of approximately two hours, and several times more lorries whined by. Occasionally they heard men calling to each other in a language they did not understand. King fancied it was French, but he could not be sure. Apart from such noises, the day passed uneventfully.

When night came, they set about making their hiding-place more comfortable, collecting brushwood and cutting long grass with their commando knives to spread at the bottom of the hollow. This at least made their bed for the night considerably drier.

King was of the opinion that they should be reasonably safe for the night. They were lucky to have arrived at the copse without anything going wrong, he said, and now it was necessary to get as much sleep and rest as possible before attempting any more sabotage. Each admitted that he was extremely tired, and King said he thought they might risk not taking turns keeping awake during the hours of darkness. It was worth risking because they must be fresh and lively for whatever they might decide was their next move. Tired men, he said, more readily made mistakes and tended to lose sight of the necessity for caution.

'We mustn't give the Boche any more chance of getting us than they have already,' he warned.

They were by this time more accustomed to the idea of being alone and to a large extent helpless in enemy territory, and that night both slept soundly until they were awakened by the 8 a.m. train rattling past. Later what sounded like half a dozen lorries trundled by.

After that nothing was heard for more than an hour and they crawled to the side of the copse on which the road lay. They remained there, lying on their stomachs in long grass, until another train came. They watched it pass in the distance – more than two miles away, they thought. Now at least they knew where the railway line was situated.

Returning to the hollow, now officially christened 'The Hole', they ate the last of their bread, washing it down with water. They noted that their water-bottles were now about half empty. The bread was very stale, but because of their hunger, and after the grass they had tried to eat the previous day, it tasted delicious.

In the afternoon, as on the previous day, they heard the sound of men calling to each other. This came from the side of the copse away from the road and nearer the village. They crawled in that direction and carefully looked out from behind a screen of bushes. Not far away from them a number of peasants were working in the fields. They were very roughly clad, and on their heads they wore black berets. They also heard the dogs barking again. The sound appeared to come from the direction of what must be a farmhouse, the roof of which they could see several fields away. It must be the dogs they had heard before. The two invaders were not greatly worried about the workers, but they were apprehensive lest the dogs on some future occasion accompanied the men to the fields and sniffed them out.

But they had slept better and were imbued with greater enthusiasm, and they began to make plans again. That night they would leave the copse for a time to make a general reconnaissance of the area and if possible single out a target for further sabotage. The operation must also incorporate a foraging expedition. It was essential that they search for drinking-water with which to refill their bottles and for something they might be able to eat, if possible to stock The Hole with some sort of food.

14 — On the Move

Night came with heavy clouds massed in the sky, and for the amateur invaders it created a welcome blackness. Most of the countryside was blotted out by darkness, as they hoped they were themselves as they moved out from the copse.

They left nothing in The Hole in case the copse chanced to be the subject of a search, stowing all their equipment in haversacks, packs and pockets. The tree-branches they placed in a different spot, dispersing the cut grass and brushwood in various places and leaving no trace of their occupation of the place.

They crossed a field and a road and continued on through open countryside, making for the direction in which they had spotted the trains passing by. After a time, they realised that the railway line must lie further away from the copse than they had judged – or they were moving in the wrong direction in the darkness. Among their other effects they had brought their compass when they left the boat. King took it out of his haversack.

'Damnation!' he swore. 'Can't read it in this light, and if we're not careful, we'll go in circles and we'll never reach the railway line.'

'Can we risk lighting a match?' asked Cuthbertson.

'I wouldn't like to,' replied King. 'What we need is an electric torch. We could have masked the light and switched it on inside our tunics. What a couple of fools we are. A torch would have been the easiest thing to acquire – and to bring with us.'

'Why didn't we think of it?'

'The fallibility of the human brain – or something like that, Leslie. Well, it can't be helped.'

They moved forward in what they hoped was a straight line across open country, crossing a couple of roads and wriggling through hedgerows. Before them a dark mass appeared in the gloom. It looked like a building of some sort, and as they drew nearer, it proved to be a farmhouse and outbuildings.

'Move off to the left,' said King. 'We'll give that place a wide berth.'

'Food,' said Cuthbertson.

'Food?' echoed King. 'What's got into your brain now?'

'Those barns near the farmhouse. There could be food in them. Turnips, potatoes, something to eat maybe.'

'I've no doubt, but we're not going to find out. If there's a dog there, it could raise hell, and we might be discovered. Make a right mess of our reccy, wouldn't it, and raise an alarm too.'

'We must take some risks to get some food,' urged Cuthbertson. 'God, man, we're starving.'

'You've got a point there, Les. But I'd like to find that railway line first. We've got work to do. Perhaps we'll take a look on the way back.'

At last they came to the brink of an embankment, and below them lay the railway line. Lying on their stomachs and peering down, they could just make out the steel tracks.

They lay for some time in complete silence before edging their way downwards. Gaining the track, they moved along it, listening intently for the sound of an on-coming train and watchful for a sign of any building or human life. Eventually the line passed out of the embankment and ran on through flat country with trees on one side.

Without warning, a small flare of light lit the darkness ahead. They halted at once. They recognised the tiny flare as a match being struck, and in the glow, prolonged for a few moments, they saw the gleam of two German-type helmets. Not thirty paces away two enemy soldiers were lighting cigarettes.

The two British soldiers stood very still for a moment, breathing deeply and watching the cigarette-ends glow brighter every time the men ahead drew on them. The Germans must have been standing still and not talking, and had they not decided at that moment to have a smoke, the invaders would have stumbled right on them.

Cuthbertson saw King loosen the flap of his pistol-holster, and he did likewise. They heard the two Germans

The December Class of the Army Dental Corps, Aldershot, 1941: Sergeant Peter King at centre, front row; Private Cuthbertson front row, fourth from right

right and below:
Pencarrow Head near Fowey where the equipment was hidden before the raid

opposite page:
Polperro Harbour – with the tide going out

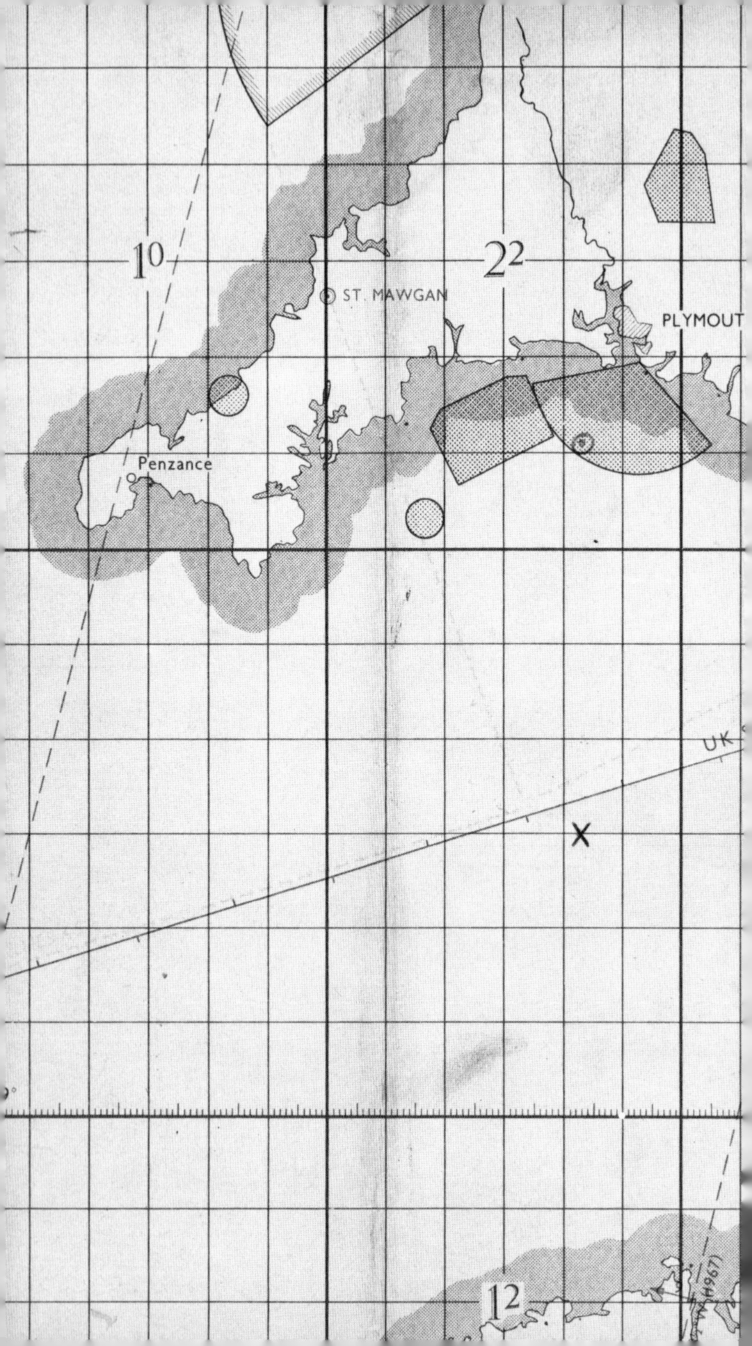

10
22
ST. MAWGAN
PLYMOUT
Penzance
UK
12

'Tinker' Bell and the crew

left: The RAF chart plotting 'Tinker' Bell's plane's lifesaving mission

Leslie Cuthbertson's presentation to 'Tinker' Bell twenty-five years after the event

Major Morton. 292

I think this is rather a good end to this story. They are not being executed & are getting what they want — after I imagine a little detention! [illegible] 6/8

G/580 5th August, 1942.

Dear Brown,

You will no doubt have seen the answer the Secretary of State gave in the House on 28th July about the famous case of Serjeant King and Private Cuthbertson of the Army Dental Corps.

You may like to know that Serjeant King has now been posted to the Commando Depot and Private Cuthbertson has been transferred to the Durham Light Infantry.

Yours sincerely,

[illegible signature]

F.D. Brown, Esq.

Major Morton's reaction to the men's sentences

Leslie Cuthbertson with his bride May Forster on their wedding day 24 June 1945

Major Morton during his term as Deputy Lord Mayor of Newcastle-upon-Tyne

Leslie Cuthbertson shortly after the time of the raid

begin a guttural conversation, and an easy laugh echoed down to them. It became obvious that so far the Germans were unaware of their presence.

Carefully King and Cuthbertson lowered themselves into the long grass at the side of the track. Making no move and not the slightest sound, they lay there watching and waiting.

One of the Germans spoke a few words, and the other answered briefly, but the men hiding in the grass, unfamiliar with the language, did not understand what was said. Then the Germans began to walk towards them.

They drew level at the other side of the railway lines and passed on, tramping up the track. The scuff of their boots on the ground grew less distinct and finally died away altogether.

King and Cuthbertson rose from the ground and made their way cautiously towards the spot where the two Germans had been standing. At that place they found a set of lines branching off the main line and leading to a siding or yard. Nearby stood a small wooden hut. The door was slightly ajar, revealing a narrow strip of light. The sergeant suggested that Cuthbertson remain concealed while he investigated the hut. He then crept towards it, approaching it from the rear, rapped hard on the wood and immediately dropped down among some bushes. No one came out, and there was not a sound inside. He beckoned Cuthbertson, and together they pushed the door open. There was no one inside.

The cabin was lit by an oil-lamp standing on a ledge and furnished with little more than a wooden stool and an empty box turned upside down.

'Look!' Cuthbertson almost gasped the word. He pointed to the ledge. On it, next to the lamp, lay an open paper parcel containing a number of thick sandwiches.

'Manna from heaven!' said King, his eyes gleaming.

Cuthbertson counted the sandwiches. 'Seven,' he said.

'Can't fool you when you're hungry,' remarked King, grinning. 'You're dead right – seven.'

'Three and a half each,' suggested Cuthbertson.

Their impulse to grab the parcel and make off with it was

short-lived. Despite his hunger, Cuthbertson said: 'Is it wise? When the food is missed, would they wonder who was starving?'

King said glumly: 'I was thinking the same. By now our boat could have been found. Someone may have seen us nosing in to land. Please God that hasn't happened. But if it has – could they think the sabotage to the wires was done by whoever was in the boat? And connect that with some hungry bastards visiting this hut?'

They made to leave but turned to look again at the sandwiches.

'One each, eh?' suggested Cuthbertson. 'A thief would be expected to take the lot, and whoever owns the food might never miss a couple.'

'Right,' said King.

Each grabbed a sandwich and stuffed it into a pocket before leaving the hut hastily and lying flat in grass some distance away.

The hut, they decided, was a shelter for a sentry, a patrol such as they had nearly bumped into, or a railway workman. The existence of the cabin and the patrol suggested that a place of some importance, probably military, lay behind the sidings to which the junction-line led.

Cuthbertson, whose watch had a luminous dial, checked the time. The German soldiers returned together in half an hour, leaned their rifles against the hut, stood chatting for a few minutes and then began to march back along the line in the direction from which they had come.

The visitors to France remained hidden, continuing to keep watch. In another half-hour the two members of the patrol returned, again waited for a few minutes and then tramped back again up the line. It was to be assumed that the patrol repeated this drill at the same regular intervals throughout the night.

The invaders began to make their way back to the copse, resting under a hedge when they were some distance from the railway line. Each demolished his sandwich. Their hunger was such that it formed a superb meal.

They remained there for a time in whispered consultation. The junction presented an inviting possibility for their next act of sabotage, and everything pointed to its being a military target. It should be possible to damage the line by use of their grenades, and if they chose the point where the branch-line was situated, more damage could be effected by the same explosives than at another part of the main track. They would have a little less than half an hour, while the patrol was absent, in which to blow up the line. But the operation must be well planned, and they decided to wait until at least the following night.

On their way back to the copse, the farmhouse they had avoided earlier lay on their left. There was nothing growing in the fields, which were newly ploughed, so no stock of food could be gained from them. The cloud was not so heavy overhead, and the outlines of the buildings were more distinct. Cuthbertson pointed, and King nodded.

The approach was made on their stomachs. When they had crawled almost to the nearest outbuilding, they found what in the darkness appeared to be a small compost-heap. Cuthbertson, who was nearer to it than King, reached out and dug his fingers into it.

At that moment a dog somewhere near to the house set up a loud barking, and he kept his hand still. They lay very still, and eventually a man's voice was heard shouting at the animal, possibly trying to quieten it. They were relieved to hear a metallic rattling, which gave them hope that the dog was chained up in the yard.

Silence returned as the hound ceased barking, and Cuthbertson's hand continued raking in the heap at his side. His fist closed on something that felt like root crop of some kind. He held it up to what light there was, and it looked distinctly like a carrot. He thrust it into King's hand and continued his investigation, finding that there were many more in the heap. Hastily they filled every available pocket with the objects. Possibly they were vegetables considered to be of poor standard, but whatever they were, they might provide something for the two men to eat.

They wormed their way along the ground away from the farmhouse, later risking rising to their feet and moving carefully beside a hedgerow.

After a time King raised a finger. His companion listened in the darkness and detected a faint gurgling sound coming from the right. Moving in the direction of the sound, they came upon a stream. On the assumption that moving water is reasonably pure, they drank from it and also filled their water-bottles.

Having then washed their faces, the idea occurred to them that they might take the opportunity of shaving by using water from the stream. Groping in their packs, they produced soap and their razors and proceeded to scrape at their faces in the darkness.

The fact that they had not crossed the stream on their way to the railway line must mean, they thought, that they were off-course on their way back to the copse. This proved to be true, and they spent some time finding their way back, eventually arriving at the clump of trees from a different angle.

Back in the Hole, with branches pulled over them and the early light of 3 May filtering through the trees, they took stock of their night's work.

They emptied their pockets of the articles they had found near the farmhouse. These proved to be carrots that had no doubt been thrown on to the rubbish heap because they were (obviously) not the best of the crop. But if they cleaned them in the stream, they found they would provide some much-needed food. The sandwich each had eaten earlier and the water they had drunk at the stream, together with the fact that they had shaved their faces, combined to raise their spirits higher than they had been for some time.

In addition, they were excited at having found what they believed was a suitable place at which to continue their sabotage efforts.

It was with some satisfaction that they settled down to rest throughout the hours of daylight, ready to move out again when darkness came and to attempt to put their latest plans into operation.

15 — Sabotage — and Flight

The invaders spent the day lying-up in the copse and working out a strategy for the night's sabotage attempt. They aimed to be in position at about midnight, hiding beside the railway near where the branch-line curved off it.

They would wait until the patrol had come to the hut, turned about and disappeared again, then wait five minutes so that any sounds they made might not be heard by the Germans. After they had done their work, they hoped to be out of the immediate area and on their way back to the copse before the patrol returned, no doubt in a hurry.

Before dusk fell, they transferred their grenades – they had three each – from the bottom of their packs to their haversacks so that they would be ready to hand. They must take care, they realised, to leave nothing at the scene which might provide a clue as to who had perpetrated the sabotage.

They stuffed their khaki forage-caps into their packs, to prevent the possibility of their falling off at the junction, and wore instead knitted, woollen balaclava helmets, which could be tucked into the necks of their tunics. The buttons on all pockets were carefully secured to prevent anything escaping from them. Using boot-polish, they blacked their faces, as they had done for their landing, checked their revolvers and made sure they were properly loaded and the safety-catches switched on.

All that remained was to obliterate all signs of their occupation of the copse, move to the edge of the trees and wait for night to fall.

Because they were keyed up and naturally apprehensive, the darkness seemed to be a long time coming, and when it did, there were indications that there would be a fair amount of moonlight, a situation they did not desire. They became edgy and a little bad-tempered with each other.

But by 11 p.m. the sky became cloudy, and the moon was

obscured. Giving each other the 'thumbs up' sign, they moved out of their shelter and made for the railway line.

They reached it without incident and waited concealed in grass and bushes within sight of the hut at which the patrol executed their turn-about. It was very quiet. There was hardly a breath of breeze to disturb the trees, and the birds had long ceased their twittering.

Eventually they heard the thud of boots on the hard ground at the side of the track, and the two soldiers of the patrol came into view. From their hiding-place, the minuscule British team had more opportunity of studying them than on the previous night. They wore steel helmets and long greatcoats, and each had a rifle with bayonet fixed slung from the shoulder. This time they entered the hut, remaining inside for a few minutes before appearing again and stepping out up the line.

If the sandwiches had belonged to them, it appeared that they had not noted the previous night that two were missing. They were relaxed, joking and laughing from time to time, apparently unsuspicious that any unauthorised person might be in the area.

King and Cuthbertson listened to their footfalls growing fainter. The patrol should, if the pattern of the previous night were repeated, be absent for about half an hour – ample time for the would-be wreckers to do their work and get clear.

A few minutes after the sound of the retreating patrol had ceased, the amateur saboteurs hurried to where the branch-line curved off into the siding. Each took two grenades and, at this stage leaving the pins in, wedged two into the crevices where lines were moved to send trains on to the branch-line. Using strong wire, they fixed the other two on to the line furthest away from the siding. The grenades thus lay in positions where each man, using both hands, could hold two at once.

The fuses in the grenades were set to seven seconds. That was precisely how long they would have to get clear after they released the clips of the grenades. They had previously counselled each other to remain cool and careful, for this allowed no time for tripping over the lines or any other object in the darkness as they hurled themselves away.

The next move was to kneel down, grasp the clips of two grenades each and extract the pins with their teeth. Then, at a signal from King, they would release all the clips simultaneously and run for it.

By listening to the rumble of trains while they hid in the copse, and timing the intervals between, they had tried as far as possible to choose a time for their attempt to wreck the line when a train might not be expected to pass. But they could not be sure that the train schedules would be the same every day, specially as the line seemed to be used by the Germans for military purposes. They would have to risk a train's coming upon them and perhaps ruining their scheme, and this was in their minds all the time they were setting their grenades in place. They were pleased that there was no sound of a train, even in the distance, as they knelt down.

The young private extracted his pins and held the clips firmly. He could see King's dark figure hunched over the line some few yards from him. It seemed a long wait, but King was making sure that his younger companion was ready.

"OK?' he called softly.

'Yes,' replied Cuthbertson.

'Now!'

They released the clips, scrambled to their feet, hurled themselves to the side of the track and began to sprint. They could not at that moment be concerned with hiding themselves or with the clatter of their boots on the stony ground, but only with getting away fast.

A moment before the explosion they were conscious as they ran of a shout behind them and the sound of running feet. Then the grenades burst. They made quite a shattering noise, the flashes lightening the darkness around them as they dropped to the ground in an attempt to avoid any splinters of iron hitting them.

It was all very satisfying to them, but they were not to enjoy it for more than a few seconds. Two men, no doubt the German patrol, were running towards them from a short distance up the track.

It did not seem possible that they had taken half an hour to fix and explode the grenades. They were never to know if this was so, or if for some reason the patrol had returned sooner than usual on this occasion. There was no time even to glance at their watches, then or for some time.

There were other explosions now, not blasts like their own splitting grenades but the sharp crack of rifle-fire. There was still some distance to run to reach the shelter of the trees and bushes which lay back from the railway line, and if the German soldiers had any skill at all with their rifles, they could pick off the wreckers even in the dimness of the night.

The British raiders made a run for it, but bullets were whining very close. Half-way to the trees, they turned to face the enemy, dropping on one knee to reduce their height as targets, and pulling at the flaps of their holsters. King took aim and fired, but the fastener on Cuthbertson's holster was sticking. Eventually he got it open and joined the sergeant in returning the Germans' fire.

It was too dark for accurate shooting, specially with pistols, but the rifle-shots ceased. Perhaps a lucky shot had winged one of the Germans. They sprang to their feet and made another dash for cover.

But the rifle-fire began again, and it seemed to be two guns as before. Again sergeant and private turned and opened fire, aiming roughly in the direction from which the rifle-fire had come.

When their pistols were empty, rifle-bullets were still coming their way. King shouted something, but Cuthbertson could not at first make out the words. Eventually he heard the word 'grenades'. The two men thrust their revolvers into the holsters and reached into their haversacks for the one remaining grenade each still possessed.

King hurled his grenade first. Cuthbertson followed suit within a few seconds. One burst beyond the line, lighting the scene brilliantly. The line was mangled and twisted. They had made a most satisfactory job of wrecking it. The other bomb showed by its flashes that it had exploded near to the wooden hut. The two Germans were at least twenty paces from where the nearest grenade burst. Their figures were plainly illuminated in the momentary light. And they were still standing.

If neither of the Germans had been hit, the exploding grenades had at least shocked them sufficiently to halt their shooting. The saboteurs raced on and crashed thankfully into the undergrowth beneath the trees. They did not pause to look back or listen but ran forward through the trees, panting with excitement and exertion. Without pausing to see what might be beyond, they raced straight out of the cover of the trees at the other side of the spinney. The caution they had displayed until then had vanished. But they were lucky: before them lay a stretch of completely deserted countryside. They ran across a field, wriggled through a hedge and crossed another field.

The Germans patrol would raise the alarm, even if the explosions and shots had not already done so. There seemed only one thing to do – put as great a distance between them and the scene as quickly as possible. To look for a hiding place was out of the question, for a wide area around the wrecked line would very soon be methodically combed by the enemy. For perhaps a quarter of an hour, they ran as fast as they could, caring little how much noise they made, thinking only that they must do their utmost to evade capture and, no doubt, subsequent death. Despite the fact that they wore British uniforms, they feared being treated as spies.

After about a quarter of an hour they settled down to a methodical jog-trot. After some further running they threw themselves down under a hedge and lay recovering their breath. But they were not to be allowed much respite.

From behind them, from the direction of the scene of their operation, came the noise of urgent activity. The night was no longer quiet as the dark countryside burst into life. They could make out the unmistakable grinding and movement of vehicles, voices shouting in the distance, motor horns echoing and the thin wail of a distant siren. The hunt was on.

To their excited and apprehensive minds it sounded like a whole regiment assembling, as though reinforcements were pouring in to the point at which they had blown up the line. There was little doubt that they had been seen as British soldiers by the two patrolmen. In a matter of minutes their roles had therefore changed from assault to retreat and from saboteurs to fugitives. It was impossible to deny the fact.

As they lay panting under the hedge, they tried to think of the best action to take. Where was their copse? After the exchange of fire with the patrol and their wild dash away from the scene, their sense of direction was impaired. In any event, to use the copse as a hiding-place was no longer advisable; it was too near the scene of the explosion. They still had an approximate idea of where the coast lay – fortunately for them in a direction roughly away from where the enemy were assembling.

A brief lull in the clamour gave them a few moments for consultation and thought. But then the noise of moving vehicles and distant shouts started up again, coming nearer as though in pursuit of them.

The fugitives reloaded their revolvers and replaced them in the holsters. Then they rose and peered over the dark countryside. They could as yet see nothing. No movement, no figures, no lights. The wind was blowing colder, but it refreshed and invigorated their minds. There was only one thing to do: run and keep running away from the noise of pursuit.

They set off at a trot, using what cover they could find, which was not much. After a time they believed that they were still ahead of the search and hoped that the German vehicles searching the roads were moving away from their own cross-country route.

Their imagination was heightened by apprehension. They might keep ahead of men beating the countryside on foot, but worry about the progress of vehicles on the roads was inescapable. Were these lorries, they asked themselves, carrying troops to places ahead of them to unload them at points from which they could comb backwards across the fields that lay ahead? If that were so, they could be caught between two forces. Would they end up trapped by an efficient pincer-movement?

At last, as they ran on, their fears appeared to have been well-founded. Precisely the same sounds as those they had heard from the direction of the wrecked railway line began to come also from the direction in which they were moving. And there were two new noises: one was the high-pitched buzz of motorcycles, the other the bark of dogs. They knew that it was said that the Germans were very thorough and efficient in anything they undertook. It appeared they were learning to their cost the truth of this belief. It was, moreover, highly likely that the enemy knew the approximate area in which they now ran, panting like foxes at the mercy of the hunt, and that soon the packs coming from in front and behind would close in.

The unpleasant thought came to Cuthbertson that the name they had given to their secret operation was all too apt, and that they were themselves like wild dogs being mercilessly hunted down.

16 — Back to Sea

Unable to go forward or back, the two fugitives turned their flight to the left, hoping they would not move towards a third and further enemy 'front'. They hoped that this might also lead to the coast, though they had not been completely certain that their original route would take them there. All they knew was that to have turned right would almost certainly have taken them inland.

If they were in fact still making for the coast, they had little conception of how far they would have to run to reach it, or of the number of roads, no doubt well-patrolled by that time, that they would have to cross in the process. What they could do if they reached the sea was a problem that must be left until they got there. They just had a sense that until they got there to flee one way was preferable to the other.

Tiring visibly, running almost automatically, willing themselves to keep on and evade capture, they had no opportunity to discuss the matter or think of their predicament in any detail. Cuthbertson at that time held on to a rather vain hope that they might find their abandoned boat, though he realised that to reach the coast at that particular spot would be in the nature of a miracle. They were firmly in the hands of capricious fate. He wondered if they might perhaps come across another boat, like the one they had tried to take in Polruan Bay back in Cornwall. Like his older companion running at his side, he had to hold on to some kind of hope.

He was gasping for breath and had a sharp pain in his chest. He wondered how the older man, who had admitted to having flat feet, was faring. One thing could not be denied: they must soon reach the point of exhaustion. They were so spent that a tuft of grass or a stone was sufficient to throw them off balace. Sometimes one stumbled, and the other helped his comrade to his feet.

Eventually, realisation of one fact brought them a few

moments of relief and hope: the noise of pursuit seemed further behind them. Gratefully they took the chance to throw themselves on the ground and take a very brief rest. Among the noises of pursuit the one that unnerved them most was the barking of the dogs; if the animals were well-trained, it must be only a matter of time before the beasts pinned down their position or reached them first and savaged them.

When the fugitives regained their breath, they consulted the luminous dial of Cuthbertson's watch. Soon dawn would break. They had no means of knowing how far they had run, but they agreed it could not have been much less than ten miles, and at a speed greater than any school cross-country event.

They remained on the ground only long enough to suggest to each other that perhaps, when the two waves of beaters met each other, they had paused to assess which way their quarry had turned. This seemed the only reason for the noises seeming a little further away.

When they rose and began to run on again, the rest seemed to have highlighted their exhaustion and weariness. Moving forward was even more painful.

By luck rather than knowledge they had chosen a flight-path that did lead to the coast. Not much further on, they reached it at last, finding themselves on a cliff-top looking out over the dark water. It was on the cards that the German coast look-outs had been alerted, and they dropped flat, wriggled forward to the edge and peered down.

It was certainly a different part of the coast from the one at which they had landed, for below and slightly to the right lay what looked like a village. Was it a fishing-village? Would there, as Cuthbertson had hoped earlier, be boats on the beach? If there were, would they be unguarded?

It was very similar to the night on which they had looked down on Polruan beach from the headland – with the important difference that their situation was infinitely more dangerous, and finding a boat was much more urgent. Then they had been soldiers in their own country absent without leave; in France they were hunted by an outraged enemy, in a war where life was not put at too high a price. The noises of the military alert were, furthermore, growing nearer again.

At the village all seemed quiet and dark, but, as they stared down, it, too, came awake. The noise of a motorcycle came to them from nearby, and the vehicle seemed to stop at the village. A motor car engine was started and then moved out. They could see what appeared to be cigarette-ends glowing in the darkness.

They must descend to the beach, said King. It was their only course of action. What they would do when they got down, they did not know, but they felt with their toes for the first foothold and began the descent.

The noise of pursuit was becoming louder and included the sound of motors. There was no time to take much care as they descended, and eventually both slipped and fell. They were in luck, however, because half-way down, the cliff became a sandy slope, and hitting this they slithered unharmed for the rest of the way down. When they picked themselves up on the beach, they could make out dark figures on the cliff-top above them, and what looked like a lorry that had been driven over the grassy headland. Shouts drifted down to them.

Then, suddenly, a searchlight stabbed down on to the beach from the vehicle. Some distance down the coast to the east another searchlight sprang to life, then another about a quarter of a mile to the west. All three proceeded to rake the sand and the sea, searching no doubt for either men or boats.

They were trapped by the sea at one side and the enemy on the other. But the nearest searchlight had done them a good turn, even though the danger of its existence was incalculable. It showed them, not far away, in a bay near to the village, a number of boats moored to stanchions. And, unlike that night at Polruan in Cornwall, they were floating.

There was perhaps one very slim chance of escape. So far as they could see, there were no craft on the sea, not near to them at least. There was therefore one way to go, one way only, into the sea. They must try to wade or swim the short distance to those boats and hope to take one before they were shot or rounded up. It would be exceedingly dangerous and its success unlikely. But desperate attempts were born of desperate situations. It was worth trying.

They waded in until they were waist high, holding their pistols above the waves, and began to move towards their objective.

Three times the beam from the nearest searchlight passed over them, casting a brilliant light over the water. After the third time the light swung back slowly, picked them out and remained trained upon them. From the cliff-top came a hail of bullets. They could hear the cracks and the whines followed by the noise of the bullets hitting the water all around them.

It seemed a miracle that they were not hit. Perhaps the searchlight was making so many dancing lights on the water that this distracted the aim of the riflemen. Maybe the soldiers had been ordered to aim wide to scare them so that they might be taken alive. Or it might just be that the incredible luck they had experienced throughout their venture still held. But why they remained alive, they would never know.

It was in desperation rather than by calculation that they raised their pistols, aiming them up the beam of light towards the lorry on which the searchlight was mounted. They were not so frantic as to think that a couple of revolvers aimed wildly at a light which dazzled them were of any use against rifles in the hands of men who could see their targets clearly. But the small weapons were all they had, and it was better to do something than nothing. They aimed directly up the beam, shooting rapidly until all the bullets were gone, sending twelve shots at the circular mouth of the searchlight.

They were astonished to find that the light went out. This was something else they did not understand. Had they hit some of the men operating the beam? Had one of their 'stray' bullets affected an important part of the searchlight's machinery? They knew nothing about such equipment, and they could not make a guess as to what had occurred.

There was a lull of less than half a minute, and then the

shooting from the cliff-top broke out again. The marksmen above were aiming in the poor light left by the extinguished beam, but there were all too many shots coming close to the British pair.

Their minds were not blank with fear, however, and Cuthbertson remembered something that had a bearing on their situation. He recalled that someone – he had forgotten who – had once told him that a bullet fired from a rifle from some distance away could not pierce water to a greater depth than nine inches. He grasped King's shoulder, pointed downwards and ducked under the surface. The sergeant followed suit, and they repeated the process several times, coming up only when they were gasping for breath.

They feared that parties of soldiers would descend to the beach and that the searchlight would flick on again, and they began to wade through the water, making for the boats. This entailed moving still deeper into the sea, and when the water was almost up to their armpits, they floundered several times. Because of the weight of their packs, boots and wet uniforms, there were occasions when they nearly drowned, swimming being impossible in the circumstances. But they were soon able to leave the water and run along a narrow strip of sand under an overhanging part of the cliff. They had to enter the sea again just before reaching their objective.

There were several lines of boats, each tied to its neighbour and the end one secured to a stanchion. Having already nearly drowned, they chose one as far out as they dared go without moving out of their depth. With their commando knives they severed the rope at each end and climbed in. It was a largish rowing-dingy, not the best of boats to attempt any lengthy voyage, but there had been neither time nor sufficient light for selection. There were four oars. They grabbed a pair each, put them in the rowlocks and began to pull directly out to sea.

They had not gone far when more noises broke out in the village behind them, including the revving of motor-vehicles, shouts, commands and the sound of a whistle being blown.

As they rowed, they had their faces towards the beach, which was still deserted, signifying that the search had not yet spilled out on to it. Soon they could no longer see the outlines of the village because of their distance from the place in the darkness. This meant, they reassured themselves, that neither could they be seen from the shore. They kept the boat moving for some time longer before risking a short rest. They were exhausted and utterly weary, both from the physical exertion of the night and from the fears that had haunted them.

Their first need was to attend to their discomforts as they were now shivering in their soaking uniforms. They took them off and wrung them out as best they could, putting them on again to dry in the breeze as they continued rowing to give some warmth to their bodies by circulation.

Lying in the boat, they held a council of war. It was 4 May. They had remained on French soil for four days.

'This is a turn-up for the book,' remarked King. 'Sounded like half a division was after us, and I bet the search is still on.'

'Can't hear a thing, Peter, can you?'

'No, but I'll bet it won't be long before we see a boat or a plane. Hope they think we're drowned, but we can't bet on it.'

'We can't stay here, that's for sure. Hope they think we were part of a larger-scale invasion and we've got them worried.'

They hauled themselves to a sitting position.

'Trouble is, we don't know where we are,' said King, unhelpfully. 'We aimed to row straight out to sea, but it's easy to go off course without using the compass. The last thing we must do is to row back towards land, not in daylight anyway.'

'The compass, Peter. Which pack is it in?'

'Mine,' said King. He searched in his pack and found it. It was still working. 'We'll assume that the northern coast of France runs roughly east to west. So we'll set a northerly course for a time, then take an east-west one.'

'Hoping for what?'

'Not hoping. Praying for night to come as soon as possible, then try to land again.'

'Into the hornet's nest again?' asked Cuthbertson.

'Afraid so. We couldn't cross the Channel in this cockleshell.'

'And we've not finished yet, Peter. If we can land and hide again, we might be able to do some more damage.'

King put his hand over the side, scooped up water and splashed it into his face. 'That's better,' he said. Taking a swig from his water-bottle, he added: 'And that's better still.'

He set the compass. 'Now, Leslie lad, let's get rowing,' he said.

When the sun was overhead, they rested and, as there was no sign of ship or plane, continued to do so for the rest of the afternoon.

With dusk they set a course west and took the oars, later turning the prow of the boat south, towards France again.

'Is there a cat in hell's chance of finding our own boat?' Cuthbertson was thinking aloud.

'That'd be just the ticket,' said King. 'It's bigger, more seaworthy – and it's got a bloody good engine. There are a few cans of petrol left aboard.'

'And the oilskins,' said Cuthbertson.

'Besides, it's the only bit of England on this coast.' King attempted a smile. 'Let's just hope the Jerries haven't found it.'

Soon it would be dawn. There was a faint pink glow in the east, spreading almost as they watched, like the explosion of a gigantic stick of bombs on the distant rim of the world. Mist lurking far away over the sea increased the loneliness of their position, and only when that cleared would there be a horizon. The sea was calm, and the boat rocked. The only sounds were an occasional creak of the boat and the gentle slap of water in the windless void. It would be a beautiful dawn.

They peered around them anxiously, but there was nothing to see – nor would there be, in the absence of ships, till the waters gleamed under the sun. They had no idea where they were or in what direction they had rowed once the land lay behind them.

They shipped the oars and lay in the bottom of the boat, conscious of an overwhelming tiredness and many aches and pains in various parts of their bodies. But their clothes were comparatively dry, and they were no longer shivering.

They judged that, after wrecking the line, they had run for a long distance roughly in an easterly and northerly direction before turning north, and if they made landfall and were lucky enough to recognise the village at which they had made their escape, then their boat would lie west of that. On the other hand, they might recognise the cliffs they had first scaled and find the *Sea Bird* there.

They rowed for a long time but saw no sign of land. Unused to navigating at sea, they could not suppress an uncomfortable feeling of being lost. They pulled on for another ten minutes, and at last they could see land. Making a landfall comforted them. It meant they were *somewhere* off the northern coast of France. They drew a little further out and settled down to wait for the night, when they hoped to fix their whereabouts more precisely.

When dusk came, they rowed in a little nearer, but nothing on the coastline seemed familiar. They struck west and, just before full darkness thought they spotted the village at which they had eluded the Germans the previous night. So in the growing darkness they rowed further west, and after about an hour they were sure they recognised the cliffs which had formed their first sight of France some days previously. They came in under the cliffs and were convinced they had found the rocky ledge where the *Sea Bird* had first touched French soil. Sure enough, a little to one side was the small inlet. Unbelievably the *Sea Bird* was still there, rocking gently where they had tied her up.

After their gruelling flight to the coast and lonely fears at sea, the sight of the boat was a tonic. They slapped each other on the back, and their tired faces creased into smiles. They wanted to shout in delight but restrained themselves in time, pointing towards the cliff-top and putting fingers to their lips.

'It's a miracle,' whispered King. 'Or Jerry has been

damned bad at searching. As little noise as possible. Gently does it.'

'Aye, aye, Captain.' It was the first time in a day and a night that Cuthbertson had felt anything like high spirits.

Very carefully, making as little noise as possible, They moved the dinghy in. On the cliff above them, as on the night they came to France, all was dark and silent. They listened intently for anything that might indicate the presence of the enemy, but there were only the sounds of sea and wind.

They thought it quite remarkable that twice they had put in at this point without being observed. One would have thought that the Germans would be more alert for their second coming. All they could believe was that this might be a stretch of coast some considerable distance from the nearest look-out station. Whatever the reason, they marvelled at their luck.

Nevertheless, they took care to make as little noise as possible as they transferred from one boat to the other. They felt better then, having more confidence in the *Sea Bird*, a larger, sturdier craft, and one which they knew had taken them all the way across the Channel.

Cuthbertson began to tie the dinghy up and leave it in place of the *Sea Bird*. But King had a better idea.

'Let's turn the dinghy upside down and allow it to drift along the coast,' he suggested. 'It will no doubt be found, and the Jerries will discover it's the one missing from the beach at that village. They'll think we stole it and that we're both drowned.'

It was an excellent ploy. They set about upturning the boat, but it seemed heavier than they thought because they were both fatigued, and they accomplished the task with some difficulty. Taking the oars of the *Sea Bird*, they rowed out to sea, giving the upturned boat a push to set it drifting.

They rowed out several miles, shipped the oars and allowed the craft to drift. Then they took turns to gain some much-needed rest, one lying in the bottom of the boat while the other kept watch.

When the glow of dawn came up over the eastern horizon, they rowed still further out to sea and stopped once more. Their hunger and thirst were intense, and they inspected their meagre store of rations. Their water-bottles were half-full, and the can in which they had brought their supply of drinking-water was about a quarter full. Turning out their pockets and packs, they found they still possessed an apple each, and that nine carrots remained from the supply they had stolen near the farmhouse. They drank most of the water from their bottles and ate an apple and a carrot each. Their plan being to sail further west and attempt a new landing in darkness further along the coast that night, they took stock of the rest of their supplies.

Ammunition for their pistols stood at just seventeen rounds. None of their grenades was left, so creating more explosions must be counted out. But they still had their stock of matches, safely stowed away in waterproof wrappings. They believed it might be possible to cause further damage by starting fires in strategic places, and other methods of sabotage might also present themselves. They might make petrol-bombs in bottles and even, hopefully steal explosives. They laid their web holsters to dry and dried and cleaned their revolvers.

The boat's tank was almost empty, and only one of their reserve cans still contained petrol, though it was less than half-full. Transferring the petrol from their one reserve can to the engine-tank, they started the motor and cruised west. After several hours the sky grew dark, and some large drops of rain pattered into the boat. Soon the craft was pitching quite steeply. It seemed certain that a storm was about to break.

The wind strengthened to gale force, and the sea heaved much as it had in the earlier part of their initial voyage to France. They had been about to cut the motor to conserve their remaining petrol, but they kept up their engine-power in order to sail into the wind and try to keep the boat as stable as possible in the gale.

When rain and wind abated, they had to admit to themselves that they were in poor plight. They had used up all their petrol. The excitements and fears of the last few days, followed by recurring bouts of seasickness during the storm, had left them in a greatly weakened condition. It must be remembered that in addition they had had little or no good food for several weeks. By this time they were both beginning to feel physically ill, and their spirits were none too high. Their optimism, a quality with which both were greatly endowed, was waning rapidly. The psychological effect of having been caught in the act of wrecking the railway line, and the subsequent hunt and flight, were beginning to have a deterring effect on their immediate ambitions. For the first time they began to doubt that two men improperly equipped and with neither backing from Britain nor assistance from the French resistance organisation, could do a great deal of harm to the enemy.

Landing on French soil again no longer appeared to be a feasible proposition, and by the next day they gave up the attempt.

The decision provided them with the bitterest moment of the venture. The quenching of their quixotic hopes, set out in their letter to Mr Churchill in terms of planning £50,000 worth of damage, was difficult to bear. Though what they had accomplished in the circumstances was quite remarkable, it is reasonable to assume, nevertheless, that no failure to complete a military target was more disappointing than theirs.

In this attitude of mind, one they found difficult to bear, they made a decision. With no petrol and only the oars for motive-power, they would try to cross the Channel back to England.

17 — Set for Home

Assuming that they were in a position somewhere near the Cherbourg peninsula, they set their compass for a route directly north. This would be the shortest way to England, and if they ever completed the trip at all, they would strike the coast well east of the Cornish village from which they had set out on the raid. But it would be a long way, impossibly long without use of their engine and with so little water and food.

By this time they were also in poor shape psychologically as well as physically to make the attempt. Once they had been willing, incredibly so, to attempt the impossible. But that remarkable spirit was draining away, and little wonder that this was so. They had not given up hope of survival, however, realising only that their raid on France was at an end and that to try to get back to England was preferable to surrendering to the enemy. That they felt a sense of failure – in this they were largely unjust to themselves – did not help. Behind them was an escapade well laced with hardship as well as danger. Before them lay a much greater ordeal and infinitely more peril. They were well aware, as they bent to the oars, that their chances of survival were very slim.

For the rest of that day they found strength to row almost continuously except for short breaks, during which they took sips of water and ate one raw carrot each, making it last by taking several bites during each rest period. They remarked on the sweetness of the vegetables and hoped that it contained some sugar to give them much-needed energy.

There had been a calm after the storm, so they had been rowing in comparatively peaceful water, and by nightfall they felt they had made reasonable progress. They had no means of knowing, however, how far north they had progressed.

Their supper consisted of a carrot each and a drink of

water. They were so weary that they found it impossible to continue rowing during the night and rested their aching limbs instead, hoping that they would build up enough energy to carry on the next day. They did not appear to be losing way by drifting, and hoped this was so. Though they were conscious of intense physical discomfort, the worst feature of that night was the overwhelming sense of loneliness brought about by the fact that there was nothing to be seen but the moving sea, dark and gleaming in moonlight. They had felt lonely and at the mercy of the sea on their way over, but then they had possessed the driving-power of their engine, and they had been full of ambitious hopes.

Later the sun shone, and the water sparkled. By midday it became quite warm. This was pleasant until it made their thirst worse.

'What about a dip in the sea?' King suggested. 'It might freshen us up a bit and get the blood going.'

'Good idea,' agreed Cuthbertson. 'It'll be damn cold, but we might feel great afterwards.'

'One at a time though. Can't leave the boat unmanned. I'll go in first and keep near the boat.'

King stripped off, lowered himself into the water and swam round the boat. 'It's great,' he shouted. 'You'll enjoy it.'

'Watch out for sharks,' laughed Cuthbertson. 'They'll bite your ruddy leg off.'

'They're waiting for your turn,' King called back. 'They're partial to Geordies.'

Cuthbertson helped his companion to climb aboard, then he went in, swam round the craft, floated on his back and with his hand sent splashes of water in the direction of King. Both aboard again, they found a towel in a haversack and rubbed themselves down. They felt invigorated and sufficiently heartened to indulge in a joke-telling session.

But later that day they realised that the exercise in the water had overtired them because of their already weakening condition.

They admitted to each other that they had used up

energy they badly needed for rowing. They did not attempt to swim in the days that followed.

To counter their depression, they tried singing together all the songs they could remember, but after a time they seemed to lack the strength for even vocal activity. They tried to sleep, but strangely they were not at all sleepy, despite the tiredness of their bodies.

When dawn came, they felt a little better. It was the second day of their ordeal adrift, and they worked out that it was 6 May.

They began the day with some show of enthusiasm by shaving themselves, using sea-water and one of the bars from the stock of soap they had brought with them. Their thirst and hunger were so great that, after drinking about half a cupful of water and eating a carrot each, the two conditions were scarcely alleviated. Nevertheless, despite their growing weakness and discomfort, they were still holding on to threads of optimism and making every effort to be cheerful. They even shared moments of laughter, such as when they tried to make water over the side of the boat, a supremely impossible manoeuvre due to the strong breeze. It was also of some help that they were warm, for despite sea-wind, the sun was strong.

They had three carrots left and declared their determination to eat no more that day, but before the sun sank again, they were to find that resolution impossible to keep, and each demolished another of the soiled and now shrivelling vegetables.

Again they rowed for most of the day and believed they were making further progress, but they were beginning to pin their hopes on being discovered by a British ship. (Later they were to care little if they met up with a German craft.) It was a day of excellent visibility, and they were both surprised and disappointed to see no sign of either ship or plane, believing as they did that the water which separated Britain from Nazi-occupied France would be well-patrolled.

Rowing was by this time an even more painful business because they had developed huge blisters on their hands, but they kept to their task until some time in the afternoon when a strong wind developed, whipping up the sea and bringing ominous, dark clouds overhead. It was an easterly wind, no doubt bringing rough weather from the Atlantic, and very soon it brought with it a stinging rain.

When the full weight of the storm reached them, the *Sea Bird* began to roll and pitch, buffeted by both wind and waves, and they shipped the oars because they feared they might lose them and because rowing had become impossible. Using two hands to the tiller, King tried to steer into the worst of the gale, while Cuthbertson clung to one of the seats. Later they managed to change positions. Steering was also extremely painful because of their blistered hands. When they tried to shout to each other, it was impossible to hear the words.

The storm grew worse and the sea more violent until one tremendous roll of the little boat tore Cuthbertson, who was trying to steer, away from the tiller and hurled him into the bottom of the boat. The danger of one of them being thrown overboard was thus impressed on them. Both realised that they must take steps to prevent this, for if one were left alone and adrift in the boat, they believed that the situation for him would be intolerable.

Leaving the rudder to its own devices, they lashed themselves to a seat amidships and to each other. But even after this precaution they feared that the seat might be torn away from the boat or broken up because of the manner in which they were thrown about. The ropes cut into their hands and waists, hurting and bruising them, and they were pulled about so much that they had the sensation of being winded. Eventually, through their fear, they marvelled that the little boat could take so much buffeting without being overturned or breaking up.

At last the wind moderated, and the mountainous waves grew smaller. They untied themselves.

The rain was still very heavy, and Cuthbertson took his entrenching tool, hacked out the petrol-tank from a hatch in which it was housed and managed to squeeze into it for shelter.

Eventually the rain stopped too, but they did not attempt to row again that day. What they had gone through, both physically and mentally, had taken its toll, and the storm had provided a sort of *coup de grâce*. For the rest of the day, and through the long night, they lay in a kind of stupor in the bottom of the boat.

Morning light brought them nothing to see but the same unending waste of water, grey and dark under a cloudy sky. The horizon on which nothing could be seen, was so monotonous as to be disturbing.

It was the third day of their ordeal at sea, and their condition was worsening. They could no longer deny, to themselves or to each other, that their position was critical. Their throats felt swollen; their heads throbbed; the blisters on their hands were extremely painful; their limbs felt inordinately heavy, and they were so weak that even to move about the boat was no longer a simple physical act. Each noted that the other's lips were swollen and that the eyes had a staring look.

They cut the last carrot in two, and each ate his share, but they found it difficult to swallow the food. Then they drank a little water. The water-can was empty, and there was very little left in their bottles.

Both spent some time that day wondering how long they could support life in their present predicament if no help came. But so far they kept such thoughts to themselves.

By mid-morning they made an effort to stir themselves. Taking their razors and soap, and scooping some water from the sea in a tin, they made an attempt to shave. Then they put the oars in the rowlocks, but when they began to pull, they found that their efforts were much less effective than previously. It was a heavy boat to propel in this way through the water, and it was obvious that their strength was ebbing fast. For several hours they struggled to row, but taking turns at the oars, the one who was resting trying to keep the other's attention on his task by sitting in front of him and every twenty seconds or so raising a stick and hitting a wooden seat to produce a sort of time-beat for each pull.(It was rather like the drummer employed to beat time for the slaves who rowed the galleys in times past.) Every so often the one trying to row would stop and sag forward to rest on the oars, and by consent when that happened the man who was restıng would prod him in the ribs.

It was a last effort to move the boat in tne direction of England. But they made little progress, and later in the day they were unable to continue. Later still they were unable to sit in the stern and hold their craft on course with the tiller.

The next hardship they had to encounter was excessive heat from the sun. All afternoon the sun was strong, giving them great discomfort and particularly affecting their thirst Cuthbertson crawled again into the recess he had made for himself in the petrol-tank hatch in an attempt to find some shade

Leaving his shelter with the intention of asking King if he would like to sit inside the hatch for a spell, he saw something dark in the water some distance astern. In his stupefied state he watched it idly for a time, wondering disinterestedly what it was. He asked himself if it could be a fish. If it were, it must be a large one, he thought. Could it be a sea mammal, a small whale maybe? He had no knowledge if whales or sharks were to be found in any number in the English Channel, and he dismissed the thought. The small effort involved in crawling out of the hatch had so tired him that he sat on one of the seats amidships, still looking astern. The thing he had seen was still there, and slowly he realised that it could not be a fish of any sort. Whatever it was, it was *floating*.

What might float in the middle of the Channel? A buoy? An excitement gripped him. If it were a buoy, that could indicate they were near to land.

He rose unsteadily and made his way to the stern where King was sitting, resting with his back to the after end and covered with an oilskin to keep the worst of the sun's rays at bay. He touched his comrade on the shoulder, and the sergeant looked up bleakly.

'What's that?' asked Cuthbertson

'What's what?' answered King without interest.

'For Christ's sake, Peter, look!'

By this time, when they spoke, their voices croaked as though they had a sickness of the chest or throat.

Slowly King turned round to look in the direction to which his companion pointed.

Cuthbertson was already realising what the object might be before King struggled up and looked hard at it.

'A mine!' exclaimed King. 'God almighty – a bloody mine.'

The thing was drifting close to them, no more than 300 yards away, bobbing and turning in the swell, its deadly antennae jutting like fingers from its rounded, rusty surface. What was more, as they gazed, the thing seemed to follow them wherever they drifted.

This was a fear, one of greater imminence than of dying from lack of water and exposure in their open boat, and it gave them enough energy to take action. They put out the oars and tried to pull away from the mine, but they were too weak to move the heavy boat far or fast enough from the floating bomb. They turned their craft first to starboard, then to port, but still the mine seemed to maintain its 300 yards distance. It was uncanny, though the truth was that they were unable to move the boat from it. Utterly exhausted, they shipped the oars.

They kept their eyes on the mine, mesmerised by it, and in time it appeared that they were drifting even closer to it. It became necessary to take further action, for on no account could they allow the boat to strike the mine.

The only thing to do, they decided, was to try to explode the mine while they were still some distance from it. They might take some of the blast, but that would be better than bumping into it.

With some difficulty, because of their swollen and blistered hands, they began to load their pistols. Each managed to squeeze three rounds into his weapon. They aimed at the mine, hoping to hit one of the antennae, and fired six shots between them. The noise of the shots seemed very loud in the almost silent day, and they could hear the bullets pinging off the mine, but the movement of the boat and the condition of their hands did not allow for good shooting, and they failed to hit any of the mine's nerve-spots. The rusty, menacing object continued to float, making a gurgling, splashing sound which they could hear distinctly because they were drawing very near to it.

They took up their oars again and made further and more frantic efforts to keep clear, but it seemed that the swell was intent on bringing them nearer to disaster. At one time they came so near to the mine that they shipped their oars in case they struck it. It was a dreadful moment.

Then slowly the mine started to bob away from them, as though suddenly the movement of the waves had changed. The gap between it and their boat widened to what it had been when Cuthbertson had first spotted it. But it never moved further than 300 yards.

For the rest of the day all their efforts were engaged in trying to keep their distance from it, mainly by trying to steer away from it with the tiller, but hour after hour it was a case of drawing near to it and then drifting away from it again.

Because of the existence of the mine they feared the coming of night more than at any time since they tried to sail north. When the light began to fade, Cuthbertson put their fear into words.

'When it gets dark we won't be able to see the mine,' he said. 'What do we do then, Peter?'

'Say your prayers,' said King.

By common consent they decided that it was better not to discuss the predicament further, but they watched the mine until it became a shadow in the darkening night, and then until it disappeared altogether. It was just about as black a night as they had experienced so far, and they could see no more than a few yards of water.

As the hours passed, they kept listening intently for the sound the mine made in the water. But curiously enough, when they could no longer see it, they found it impossible to distinguish the swishing of the mine from the slap of water on the sides of the boat. Every moment they expected to bump into the infernal thing. It was a long night.

It was almost dawn before sleep overcame their fears and they lay in an exhausted slumber in the bottom of the boat.

18 — Ordeal

The sun was bright when they awoke with a start to the realisation that they should not have allowed themselves to fall asleep. Apparently the mine had not exploded, but they were anxious to know how near to it they were.

Taking great care not to rock the boat, they hauled themselves from a lying position on to their knees and peered over the gunwale. It was not at that side. Slowly they moved aft on hands and knees. It was not astern of the boat. Rising to their feet, they looked all round, first in the vicinity of their craft and then into the distance. It was nowhere to be seen. Some time during the night, quite incredibly, it had disappeared.

They made no attempt to think what had caused the mine to vanish, to work out what wind and tide had done to take the boat and the dangerous floating bomb in different directions. They were only too pleased to find themselves removed from the hazard.

Their relief found expression in laughter. It was no more than a dry cackle from their parched throats and cracked lips, but it was laughter. They made a weak attempt to slap each other on the shoulder and gave a 'thumbs up' sign, and though nothing they had done themselves had removed the mine from the vicinity, they gave each other a congratulatory handshake.

When King had suggested, the previous evening, albeit in a laconic manner, that there was nothing left except to pray, Cuthbertson, the ex-Church Lads' Brigade NCO, the former devout church-goer, had done precisely that. Alone in the cupboard he had made of the hatch, he had asked seriously and sincerely for deliverance from that particular peril. That morning, when they laughed because they were still safe, they became very solemn and thoughtful, sitting down and bending their heads forward. Cuthbertson did not know if his companion was praying, but he was certainly doing so, his hands clasped before him, giving thanks for what he believed was divine intervention for their safety.

Now that the mine had disappeared, their spirits rose higher than they had been for some forty-eight hours. They splashed sea-water in their faces and made another attempt to shave, a painful operation because not only their hands but their faces were now affected by their privations. But when the task had been accomplished, they felt better for it.

They took a few sips from their water-bottles and then shook them – to find no sound inside. All their water-supply had gone. The discovery was unpleasant, but at that moment it did not cause too much worry, the deliverance from the mine being looked upon by them both as a sign that perhaps they would survive their ordeal.

For some time they had made no attempt to keep a mental log of the number of days they had been adrift. Up to then their ordeal in the boat had lasted only a few days, yet it was astonishing and disconcerting to find that it was not so easy to decide how much time had elapsed since they had escaped to sea from the French coast. Each day since had been similar, monotonously so.

'What day is it?' croaked King.

'Tuesday – no, Wednesday. I don't know. I don't care either.'

'Not the day, you clown,' said King making a gesture of impatience because his voice was too hoarse to imply it. 'The date, idiot.'

'Don't know. Does it matter, Peter?'

'It damn well does. We've got to keep track of time.' From time to time they were getting snappy with each other. 'We mustn't get so we don't care about *anything*.'

Cuthbertson pulled himself out of a spell of day-dreaming. 'Got what you mean! Like Robinson Crusoe kept a tag of the days?'

They forced themselves to think of any events which might fix the date. King remembered that on the day they had decided to search for and transfer to their own boat he had noted that the date was 4 May, having worked out then that they had been four days on French soil. The next day, they recalled, they had found the *Sea Bird,* suffered a storm at sea and afterwards decided to make for England. So that must have been 5 May. How many days had elapsed since? On 6 May they had managed to row all day. The next they had encountered the mine. The present day must, therefore, be 8 May. Four days so far, and it had seemed like twice that number!

King took the entrenching tool and scored a mark on the wood of the stern seat. Under that he scratched a rough figure eight, and put four marks to the left of the one the date referred to. Each day, he said they would make a fresh mark.

By that day they had no strength whatsoever to use the oars, and from that time on they were to find rowing quite impossible. In the days that followed they were to leave the boat to drift as it would.

It was a very bright morning, and by this time their eyes were beginning to give them trouble. They were not able to stand the light of the sun, and for long periods they kept their eyes closed. At times they fell asleep and at others gazed listlessly over the side of the boat. At night they curled themselves up in positions where they might gain some shelter from the cold wind. In this way the days and nights passed, intolerably slowly and with bodily and mental suffering.

On the sixth day it rained, not this time in a stormy manner, and they rigged up a waterproof groundsheet in such a way as to collect the rainwater. It took a long time for any amount to build up in the middle of the sheet, the rain being fairly light, but it did rain for several hours, and when it ceased, they moved forward eagerly to transfer the water to their bottles. It was two days since their supply had given out and since they had had even a sip of water.

As they carefully put forward their bottles, the boat, caught by a big wave, lurched suddenly and all the water spilled out. It was a dreadful sight as they gazed at the precious liquid spreading over the floorboards of the boat. They stumbled forward and tried to lick moisture from the wet groundsheet, then from the floor of the boat, but they gained no more satisfaction than moistening their lips.

Slowly they rose to their knees and sat staring bleakly at each other, as though the ordeal of their days adrift had now completely undermined their spirit.

At last the muscles of King's face began to move, as if he ground his teeth, and his eyes looked like those of a man who habitually wore strong glasses and had just taken them off.

'I think – maybe – our luck is beginning to run out,' he said, and his voice was little more than a whisper.

Cuthbertson looked at him as though drowned in apathy. Then, for a brief moment, he gave vent to his feelings, not in words but by picking up the entrenching tool and battering at the pieces of the petrol-tank he had previously hacked out of the hatch.

Later it began to rain again. Quickly they rigged up the groundsheet, praying that the rain would continue for a long time. At last there was sufficient water in the hollow of the sheet for them to lay one water-bottle flat in it and collect a little. This time they did not wait until the water was deep, fearing that they might again lose the lot. In this way they kept adding more to the bottle until eventually it was full.

They allowed themselves a few sips each and settled down to another long spell watching more rain collecting in their sheet. When there was just enough to transfer some to the second bottle, the string holding the groundsheet gave way and the water was lost. They cursed themselves for not having bent down and drunk the water a moment sooner rather than lose it. But again they fixed the groundsheet, knowing that persistence with this task might mean survival. At last, bit by bit, they filled the second bottle. They left the sheet in position and when the rain ceased, there was a little more water swilling in it. This they drank from the sheet, and it provided one of the most refreshing moments during their ordeal. When they had sucked it all up, they continued licking the wet sheet to gain the last particle. The water tasted rubbery – but delicious.

The whole of that day had passed gathering their new water-supply. It was time well spent, for after that it did not rain again.

During the days that followed they rationed themselves to two teaspoonfuls of water each, twice a day, later cutting it to once daily.

They became so weak that they lost the will to talk to each other. It was almost as if they preferred to lie day-dreaming.

On the seventh day they made a further attempt to assist their chances of survival by trying to bag a seagull in the hope of eating the flesh. They had had no food for four days since they ate the last carrot of their supply taken from the farmyard.

A few gulls were circling over the boat. When the birds had arrived, they had hoped they were near to land, but later they had been forced to realise that that might not be so.

One of the gulls appeared to be floating on the water not far away, and the idea came to them to shoot at it. They took out their revolvers and ammunition and found that they had eleven rounds left. They spent four bullets before hitting the bird, and bringing the boat about with the tiller. They reached out with an oar and brought it to the side. they plucked it, pierced it with a knife and drank the blood, but it was extremely distasteful, and they almost vomited. There was no way of cooking the bird, but they cut off pieces of the flesh and tried to eat it raw. It was very tough, and they were unable to swallow any of it. In disgust they threw the dead gull overboard.

The effort to gain nourishment in that way being abortive, they then conceived the idea of trying to catch a fish. They rummaged around the boat and found the fishing rods they had pretended to use while waiting to slip away from Cornwall. There was no satisfactory bait, and they tried using bits of cloth on their hooks. They persevered for hours but caught nothing, cursing themselves for having thrown the gull away, as pieces of its flesh, they believed, might have attracted the fish. By that time there were no gulls about which they might have tried to shoot.

More days passed, and though there was no great swell on the sea, they feared that they had grown so weak that any roll of the boat greater than usual might pitch them overboard. As they had done during the storm, they lashed themselves to the boat, this time to the floorboards.

They no longer made any effort to shave or to talk to each other, even in hoarse whispers. They just lay there in a state of total inertia, admitting in their own minds that hope was fading.

19 — Where Are They?

During the time the two soldiers drifted helplessly in the Channel further enquiries and investigations into their disappearance were taking place in Britain.

Following the court of enquiry at Aldershot about the missing arms and ammunition, a record of those proceedings was being studied by various Army authorities. Though the court had recorded no opinion about the loss of the weapons, those who read the evidence given to it did have the view, confidently expressed by Lieutenant-Colonel S. H. Woods, commandant of the Army Dental Corps School of Instruction at Aldershot, and backed by the Corps of Military Police, that the two pistols and ammunition had been taken by Sergeant King.

After being furnished by Major Morton with the unofficial invaders' letter to the Prime Minister, the War Office had been busy, as Mr Churchill's personal adviser on intelligence had suggested, finding out 'whether these two gentlemen have disappeared from their unit', if there was anything further to suggest that they had really carried out their suggested intention and all that could be discovered in general about the two men.

Having made their enquiries at the Dental Corps at Aldershot, on 7 May the War Office sent a letter to Major Morton's assistant giving all the facts they had gathered. It was written on the day the two errant heroes were trying to avoid collision with the floating mine.

The letter read:

> Dear Brown,
>
> You sent to Miss Campbell on 30 April a copy of a letter from Sergeant P. King, of the Army Dental Corps, announcing his intention of setting off with Private L. Cuthbertson for a raid on Occupied France.
>
> Both men were reported as absentees on 14 April and are still absent. At the same time as they disappeared it was discovered that two pistols and forty-one rounds of ammunition held by the school at

which they were employed were missing. A court of enquiry into the circumstances has been held locally, but we have not yet heard the result.

Their Army records are as follows:

Sergeant King enlisted in the AD Corps as a clerk-orderly on 15 March 1939, on a normal Regular engagement (seven years with the Colours and five in the Reserve), date of birth is declared as 9 April 1915 but stated to be now of apparent age thirty-five/thirty-six.

No previous service declared, but had exceptional abilities as a drill-instructor, and it is believed that he had undoubtedly had some previous military or police service.

Stated that he was born in New Zealand.

Promoted A/Corporal 1 October 1939, and War Substantive Sergeant 16 April 1940.

Qualified 'D' as an instructor anti-gas.

Military conduct exemplary.

No entries in Company or Regimental Conduct Sheets.

Employed in the military training of Army Class Intakes and of officers joining on first appointment, and stated to be an instructor of outstanding ability.

Private Cuthbertson enlisted with Army Class Intake as a dental mechanic on 11 December 1941, date of birth 5 August 1922. Stated to have been an NCO and PT instructor in the Church Lads' Brigade, to be 'exceptionally keen on soldiering' and more eager to understudy Sergeant King than to work in his trade of dental mechanic.

Conduct above reproach and no entries recorded in Company or Regimental Conduct sheets.

All the evidence there goes to show that both men were exceptionally keen soldiers, and it is all consistent with the idea that they really have set off for France.

Yours sincerely,
N. G. Morrison.

F. D. W. Brown Esq.

Before passing the letter to Major Morton, Mr Brown wrote a note on it which read: 'Have you heard any more?'

These words in Brown's handwriting might have suggested that some doubt still remained as to whether the two soldiers had in fact put their intention into practice, but the suggestion that the two had really set off for France, contained in the last paragraph of the letter from the War Office, was now to be generally accepted by those enquiring into the matter.

That Major Morton was beginning with some caution to

favour this theory is evident by the note he attached to the War Office letter when forwarding it some five days later to Colonel Clarke, of the Special Operations Executive. He wrote:

13 May 1942

Dear Brien,

We have now had the attached from the War Office about the mysterious Sergeant King and Private Cuthbertson, regarding whom I wrote to you on 30 April.

The main point is that on the present evidence, admittedly thin, it is very possible that these two men have really set off for France.

Yours ever,
Desmond Morton.

Colonel Brien Clarke,
64, Baker Street,
W1

The Special Operations Executive were well-prepared to believe that King and Cuthbertson had actually set off with the intention of infiltrating unobserved into France and were already keeping alert for any news about them coming in from their agents in that country.

Colonel Clarke's assistant replied to Major Morton, stamping the letter 'Most Secret', in these words:

LONDON
19 May 1942

Dear Major Morton,

As Colonel Clarke is at present away on leave, I write to thank you for your letters of the 13 and 17 May enclosing further papers on the Sergeant King and Private Cuthbertson mystery.

All the accounts you have sent us have been shown to the Section here which looks after Occupied France, and they are keeping a lookout for any signs that these two braves actually have landed and got to work.

Naturally, if we hear any trace of them we will let you know.

Yours very truly,
B. Salt.
Assistant to Lt-Colonel Clarke.

Major Desmond Morton, CMG, MC
10 Downing Street.

The mystery appeared to be solving itself. The letter from the two soldiers, which at first had seemed astounding enough to be a hoax and still remained a remarkable document, was by this time being accepted as a sincere declaration of intent from two non-combatants who were determined to get into action – with or without permission. The army authorities were beginning to recover from the initial shock given to them by two soldiers who refused to wait for the military machine to move fast enough to provide some form of excitement for them. A hint of admiration was finding its way into some of the letters passing between investigating officers.

The two soldiers having successfully given the Army the slip and got away on their own, there was little the authorities could do but sit back and wait for some positive news about their location and what they were doing.

For the War Office, the SOE, Major Morton and all others involved in Britain, the situation contained a number of imponderables. Many things could prevent any further news of the two men reaching them, the chances being that they would not survive such an operation mounted entirely on their own devices.

There was, however, nothing to do but wait.

20 — Suicide Pact

On their tenth day in the boat, 14 May, the rain-water the two soldiers had collected gave out. The days were long and sunny, and there was no indication of a break in the weather leading to further rain. Still they had not been sighted by any ship or plane, either British or German, and there was no sign of either. If they were drifting away from any routes normally followed by warships or reconnaissance aircraft, there was nothing they could do about it because of the weakness that overwhelmed them.

The sight of each other made them more than ever aware of their physical condition. Cuthbertson found that his hands seemed thin and bony. He could not study his own face, but he could see the appearance King's presented: it was gaunt, the cheekbones standing out and the skin pale with a yellowish tinge. He noted that the sergeant's eyes possessed for most of the time a staring look compatible with lack of comprehension or despair. His own face, he knew, must look much the same, and the realisation did not help him. Their lips were dry and cracked, their throats parched, and the thirst they were experiencing seemed unbearable. The growth of a stubbly beard covering their cheeks and jaws was not only unsightly, it made their faces itch most unpleasantly.

The younger man saw that King's feet and ankles were swollen. He wondered if this might be as a result of all the running they had done while escaping from the Germans, the sergeant having what the Army termed 'flat feet'. Then he saw that his own were swollen, not so much as King's, and he was astonished that he had not been aware of it previously.

King in his turn noticed that Cuthbertson's lips were moving as he bent over clasped hands, and wondered disinterestedly what his young comrade was trying to say. (By that time each was no longer interested in any utterances made by the other.) Cuthbertson was not in fact trying to speak to him, nor was he speaking to himself, though later each had spells of doing that: he was praying for rain, to be sighted by a ship, most of all that they would survive.

The next morning their thirst was so great that they decided to save the urine they passed in a couple of tins and try to purify it with the tablets they had taken from the stores at Aldershot. Towards the end of the day they thought they had collected a sufficient quantity, and they added the tablets and drank the liquid. The experiment was not a success; they retched violently and almost vomited.

By the twelfth day they were convinced they could not support life much longer. They did their best to face this prospect, but it was one accompanied by other dreads as well as the final one of death – fears that their reason would be impaired, that madness might take hold of them and that they might commit acts leading to their own destruction.

Lying in the boat with their shoulders against the gunwale, they began at last to put into words to each other the fact that they faced the prospect of death. Apart from a few words to each other the previous day, when they had made use of the water-purifying tablets, it was the first time they had spoken to each other for some time, certainly the first discussion of any length in which they had indulged for some days. There evolved from this the recognition of what was perhaps their greatest fear of all – the chance that one would die before the other. Each realised how terrible it would be to witness the other's death and to be left alone in the boat, suffering physically and mentally, waiting for his own end.

From the despairing examination of their plight there came the idea for a macabre plan – a pact to commit mutual self-destruction at some time not far ahead when they would at last believe death to be very imminent.

They went so far as to decide how the final act would be performed – by shooting each other at the same moment, and they even carried out a macabre rehearsal, actually practising a suicide system. They looked out what remained of their ammunition – seven bullets. These they laid aside. Each took an empty pistol and sat in the boat facing the other. Pointing the weapons at each other, they began counting aloud to practise pulling the triggers simultaneously.

'One, two, three,' they said and pulled the trigger. One, two, three – click. One, two, three – click.

The strange performance went on for about five minutes. It ended when, because of his weak state, Cuthbertson could no longer sustain the effort and pitched forward into the bottom of the boat in a faint. He came to later with the pistol still in his hand, still counting and pulling the trigger. King dropped his weapon, slid on to the floorboards beside Cuthbertson, took the pistol from his hand and laid it beside his own.

After that they drew away from each other, physically, and mentally, remaining apart, each at opposite ends of the boat. They did not again move close to each other, withdrawing themselves, each within his own stupor and imagination. They were no longer a team. It was as though the dreadful aspect of the pact had severed any sense of sharing their plight.

From then on they lay in the bottom of the boat, with no desire to look over the gunwale at the sea and no hope of seeing anything on the horizon. They drifted in and out of consciousness.

When he was awake, Cuthbertson found that all the sounds around him, the slap of the water on the boat, the creaking of wood and the blowing of the breeze were transformed into imaginary voices or music. He became a prey to delusions. One was that he was being offered a cup of tea. Another was that a woman, who was vaguely like his mother, was offering him a huge portion of his favourite apple pie. Others were of a nightmarish quality.

This was the grave nature of their condition at the end of their fourteenth day afloat. If rescue failed to come by the next day, it was unlikely that they would live.

The next morning, 19 May, Whitley bomber Zebra 6734, of No. 502 Squadron, Coastal Command, was due to take part in an operational exercise with the British submarine *Thunderbolt* south of the Eddystone Lighthouse.

When the aircraft arrived over the area, the submarine was not yet in position, and the bomber's captain, Warrant-Officer W. A. Bell, whose home was at Northampton, was instructed by radio to delay the start for thirty minutes. To use up the waiting-time, the Whitley's captain, who was known in his squadron as 'Tinker' Bell, decided to make a number of outward sweeps across the Channel. During that time he and his crew kept a normal lookout but saw nothing of importance.

On the last of the sweeps Warrant-Officer Bell took the plane some distance further than on the previous occasions and reached a point which was, according to the navigator, approximately halfway to the French coast at that part of the Channel. He looked at his watch and, deciding it was time to turn back, turned the bomber in a wide arc. Then, just as he was settling down to fly the aircraft back to the operational area, the boat in which King and Cuthbertson lay was spotted below.

It appeared to be a small boat; there was no sign of life in it from the height at which the plane was flying, and it seemed to be drifting. (King and Cuthbertson were, of course, lying flat in the bottom of the boat in a stupor.)

The time was 9 a.m.; it was a clear morning, and if the boat was manned, there should have been some indication, even from that height. What was a boat of that size doing adrift in the Channel some fifty miles from the coast of England and about the same distance from France? One that had broken from its moorings on either coast? Or a ship's boat that had fallen unnoticed overboard? A number of possibilities presented themselves, none of any apparent importance, as the bomber crew believed that no one would venture into mid-Channel in so small a boat in wartime.

Warrant-Officer Bell decided, however, that he might as well take a closer look. Descending to a few hundred feet, he passed over the boat. It was seen then that two men appeared to be lying asleep – or dead – in the bottom of it.

The pilot gained height in order to come down again in another sweep over the floating craft. He believed that if the occupants of the boat had been asleep, they would have awakened quickly because of the roar of his engines. But they had not stirred, and the chances were that they were dead.

The noise of the bomber had, however, roused Cuthbertson. He struggled to a sitting position and, looking up, saw the plane above to his left gaining height, banking and circling. With the utmost difficulty, stumbling and falling, he made his way to the stern and roused King. It was the first time for days that either had ventured nearer to the other than four yards or so, or tried to communicate with the other. On their hands and knees, helping each other, they crawled to the mast and managed to raise themselves to a standing position, clinging to it with one hand and waving weakly with the other.

When Warrant-Officer Bell came down low again and passed over the boat, it was quite obvious to him and his crew that the men in the boat were alive. Furthermore, they appeared to be wearing British Army battledress.

Bell took the plane up again and circled the boat, keeping it well in sight while his navigator charted an exact position on his map. Bell then radioed his base, reporting the sighting and giving the boat's position. He was ordered to remain with it and to home a rescue Lysander aircraft and a destroyer to the position. For five and a half hours the Whitley remained overhead, keeping the boat under surveillance, until the arrival of the Lysander, which in turn circled over the boat until a Norwegian destroyer, which had been asked to help, arrived on the scene.

Meanwhile the two in the boat were experiencing a series of deep emotions – overwhelming relief that they had been found, excitement that was almost difficult to bear in their weakened condition and finally frustration that it was taking so long to get them off the boat. They knew that the Whitley and then the Lysander were RAF craft and guessed that a ship might be on its way. But with help almost at hand their thirst grew even worse. They hoped the aircraft would come in low and drop something containing water into the boat. This did not happen, and eventually, as the sun rose and the day became warmer, they were again overcome with weakness and fell once more into languor and stupor. Several times they reawakened – to be haunted each time with the terrible thought that the aircraft had been a dream or a delusion, but then came the reassuring sight and sound of the plane to save them from craziness.

It was in the afternoon that they awakened to hear, in addition to the drone of the Lysander, voices close at hand. The language being used was guttural, and they did not understand it. They raised themselves and looked over the gunwale to find that a destroyer was lying nearby and that the voices belonged to the crew of a rescue-boat heading towards them.

King and Cuthbertson looked at the destroyer almost unbelievingly. Cuthbertson recalls putting a hand on his companion's shoulder making a weak gesture towards the ship and having to struggle to compose himself to speak.

'Peter . . . we're going to be rescued,' he said with great difficulty.

At that moment both were convinced that it was a German ship, yet they were puzzled by the fact that the two planes had been obviously British.

The point where they were rescued was due south of the Eddystone Lighthouse, south-west of Plymouth and, as already stated, almost equidistant between England and France. It was some eighty miles and almost due west from the tip of the Cherbourg peninsula.

Almost certainly King and Cuthbertson had put to sea from that peninsula. Consequently they must have been unable to row any appreciable distance north towards England and had therefore drifted due west into what was later mid-Channel. They could not have been, at one time, far from the Channel Islands, passing them on their port bow, and had help not come when it did, it is likely that they would have continued drifting straight out into the Atlantic. Had the naval-air exercise not been scheduled for that day, had the submarine been in place at the right time, or had Warrant-Officer Bell chosen to use the waiting-time in flying in a different direction, there is little likelihood that the two would have been saved from death.

Before the rescue boat reached them they both collapsed, but they were lifted out of their boat and hoisted aboard the Norwegian destroyer. They came to in the ship's sick-bay, where attendants were trying to feed them with gruel from a spoon. They were helped into a sitting position so that they could see each other, and a voice said in English: 'You're all right now.'

Three of the destroyer's officers came into the room and spoke in Norwegian, but neither Cuthbertson nor King knew any other language but English, and they again believed that the men were speaking German.

'British,' Cuthbertson managed to say, and immediately fell back asleep in the bunk.

Awakening later, they found that their rescuers had brought all their equipment – their pistols and remaining ammunition, entrenching tool, wire-cutters, packs, haversacks, even the bottle of water-purifying tablets – into the room and had laid them out neatly on a table near their bunks.

One of the stewards spoke English, telling Cuthbertson that he came from Shields, which was not far from his own home on Tyneside. At first Cuthbertson believed this to be a German trick and refused to answer when a Norwegian officer asked in English: 'Where have you come from?' Eventually the British steward managed to convince the two that they were among friends, telling them that they were aboard a Norwegian destroyer which was going to put in to Plymouth. They were aware that it was a strange coincidence that they were to be put ashore at the same town in which they had written their letter to the Prime Minister and from which, after travelling there by train from Aldershot, they had set off on their adventure. Their point of disembarkation was also no more than about twenty miles across-country from the Cornish harbour from which they had put out for France.

As the ship steamed in, they were beginning to recover a little from their ordeal. They were also beginning, in a weak sort of way, to regain some of their spirits, though these were soon to be considerably lowered again.

21 — Court Martial

It was the morning of the day the two were brought in to Plymouth that the Special Operations Executive in London, unaware of their rescue at sea, were writing their letter to Major Morton at Downing Street assuring him that they were keeping a lookout for any news from their agents in France that the two Dental Corps men had 'actually landed and got to work' in that country.

When the destroyer came in, that letter had not yet been delivered, and the authorities investigating the disappearance of the two men were still much in the dark as to the situation, though most tended to support the theory that a private attack of some sort was taking place against the Germans in Occupied France. Security and intelligence branches of the Army on the spot in Plymouth were, therefore, taken rather by surprise when word reached them from RAF Coastal Command and the Norwegian destroyer that two men wearing British Army uniform had been picked up in the Channel. Their first reaction was one of extreme caution, resulting in a rough reception for King and Cuthbertson.

Considering that only the SOE operations centre and a few intelligence officers, including Churchill's special adviser, all based in London, knew that an unofficial raid on France had been contemplated or might be taking place, and that the Dental Corps at Aldershot had left the mystery of the two missing desperadoes to the War Office and the police, the severity of the reception given to the two soldiers was perhaps understandable, for the following reasons. Within a short time of the war's starting, the German spy-ring in Britain had been virtually rubbed out, and the enemy desired to remedy that situation in any way possible. One method they were using was to infiltrate a suitable agent into a French escape-party, which would be allowed to slip through their control. An alternative method was to send one or two individuals in small boats from trawlers or other small ships stealing out to within a few miles of the English coast. The result was that King and Cuthbertson were by no means the only offerings from the sea requiring the attention of the Security Service. Indeed, at that period of the war the latter were receiving quite a number of 'visitors' from France in all sorts of small craft.

Even had they been aware of this, it would have been small consolation for the two adventurers, who were supremely thankful to have survived the expedition and expected, if not a heroes' welcome, at least some praise, possibly laced with a slight ticking-off for having gone off without permission. In the event, they were carried ashore on stretchers right into the midst of an armed guard.

A doctor examined them at the dockside, and they were taken to three civilian hospitals in turn, at each of which they were given an injection, but none of which would consider allowing them to remain for a moment longer than necessary. These institutions were not military ones, and it seemed that the two unfortunate soldiers were considered too hot to handle.

At the third hospital Cuthbertson explained that they had been many days without anything to drink and asked if they might have some tea or cocoa. When the doctor who was examining them asked the hospital staff if drinks could be provided, the matron said it was 'a bit late' for this to be done, whereupon the doctor asked if she would 'try to find something for the men'. A nurse brought not a drink but a huge, thick, cheese sandwich which they could not have eaten because of the condition of their lips and throats. By this time Cuthbertson was getting understandably a little belligerent; he threw the sandwich at the nurse.

The fourth hospital they were sent to was a military one, and to this they were admitted. There the first day they were given small quantities of gruel. The following day they were given their first drink – a cup of tea. Their enjoyment of it was to some extent offset, however, by the presence of a soldier sitting beside their beds armed with a rifle, especially as the guard had been ordered not to answer any question they asked or to converse with them in any way. It was disconcerting to realise that, far from having fully demonstrated their loyalty to their country, they were being treated as dangerous characters.

There was worse to come, however. Severe and lengthy interrogation began as security officers arrived and set to finding out if they were in fact the persons they said they were or agents the Germans were trying to implant in Britain.

It soon became obvious to the two that the story they told their interrogators that they had conducted a private invasion of France on their own was not believed, nor their claim that they had written to Winston Churchill to warn him of their attempt beforehand. In fairness to the security men, of course, both these claims must have seemed astonishing. To make things worse, since being picked up by the destroyer, the two had begun to make a rapid though temporary recovery, possibly due to their self-imposed training and fitness before their ordeal. In consequence of this, the doctors reported to officers of both the Special Branch and the Security Service that their physical condition was not consistent with their having been adrift, as they claimed, in an open boat for fourteen or fifteen days.

The chief interrogator was Colonel H. L. Warner, who arrived at the hospital each day in civilian clothes. He was extremely methodical, forcing them to tell their story over and over again and picking on any slight variations of fact. Again and again Cuthbertson was asked to go over his family history, stating the name of the school he had attended, the church at which he had worshipped, the name of the vicar. That they were unable to produce their Army 64-pay-books did not help them to identify themselves satisfactorily.

It was King's and Cuthbertson's turn to be astonished – and to no small degree alarmed – to find themselves treated like enemy spies following their adventure born of such good intent, and after their ordeal in the boat.

Colonel Warner, who is not to be criticised for doing his job efficiently, made his visits alternately kindly and menacing, the latter ones invariably ending with the command: 'Right, let's have the truth now.' Eventually all his visits were friendly, the interrogations having come to an end, and they were then asked questions designed to discover if they had learned anything while in France that might be useful to the war-effort. Cuthbertson did not learn the reason for the change until some thirty years later, when he received a letter from Colonel Warner, then a Sussex businessman: the condition of the two soldiers had deteriorated again, and the doctors, then having little doubt that they were suffering from a powerful delayed action, revised their opinion and stated that their physical condition *was* consistent with an ordeal such as they described. When the security men were satisfied that there was nothing sinister in the arrival of King and Cuthbertson and consequently lost interest in them, the Army itself took over, with equal interest.

All events may seem clearer in retrospect, but it is interesting to note, for instance, that there could have been, perhaps, easier and quicker ways of establishing their identity. There were plenty of responsible people at Aldershot who could have said at once that they were who they claimed to be. Cuthbertson's family could have satisfied the authorities regarding their identity, if not the reasons for their turning up in mid-Channel. Yet none of these was asked for assistance. Regarding their claim to have sent their pay-books to Downing Street, one might have thought that this also could have been verified with reasonable speed, but it is certain that neither Major Morton at Downing Street nor Colonel Clarke at Baker Street was aware at that time that the two soldiers whose story was so fascinating had turned up at Plymouth.

They remained in hospital under armed guard for some six weeks. It was then decided to return them to Aldershot – and in a manner which demonstrated convincingly that they were still regarded as dangerous characters. Apparently the Army was still finding it difficult to regard two men who had planned a private raid on France as anything but desperate and unusual soldiers.

The sergeant of the guard, comprising eight soldiers, actually handcuffed them before the start of the journey. Explaining this move, the NCO told them: 'I'm using these because we know you are desperate characters. I must also warn you that the rifles my men are carrying will be used if there is an attempt to escape.'

The train in which they travelled had two compartments reserved, one for each prisoner and his escort. Cuthbertson was painfully aware of the stares of civilians on the platform. He was deeply conscious of and humiliated by the ignominious appearance they presented, especially when he heard a suggestion passing between two civilian travellers that they must be German prisoners. He sat down on the platform and told his guard that he would refuse to move until the crowd was told that they were not Germans. The guard hauled him to his feet to bundle him away, and he held up his manacled hands and shouted to the people on the crowded platform: 'I'm a British soldier, and this is the way they treat me.'

The handcuffs were taken off only when they were placed in separate cells at an Aldershot camp, where they were kept for about nine days in solitary confinement. They were allowed ten minutes' exercise each day, under armed guard, none of whom would speak to them. Otherwise they were not allowed out of their cells, in which were placed buckets for them to relieve themselves; their food was pushed through a hatch. There were occasional visits from an Army padre.

From time to time they were taken, handcuffed, before an officer to be asked if they had any complaints. Each time they had one in particular – a request not to be handcuffed.

On 8 July they were led to a room in the headquarters building and told they were to face a court martial. The next day they were marched, again handcuffed, into the Aldershot court-room and before the presiding officers.

As soon as Cuthbertson was taken into the room, he heard the first kind words since their ordeal at sea. They were spoken by the presiding officer.

'Why is this man in handcuffs?' he asked.

'Acting under orders, sir,' replied the escort sergeant. 'It has been the usual practice, sir.'

The court president showed annoyance. 'This is a British soldier,' he retorted. 'Remove the handcuffs at once.' He further ordered that the guard be dismissed from the room.

It appeared from the nature of the court proceedings that information and support, a little delayed perhaps, for their story of genuine desire to help the war-effort, had now been made available to those convening the trial. The War Office was in possession of the letter they had sent to the Prime Minister at the start of their expedition and also their Army Books 64. The War Office, excessively busy with the whole conduct of the war, together with intelligence officers in London, had at last found time to come to the aid of the two unfortunates in the final predicament of their strange adventure. This obviously influenced the charges they might otherwise have had to face, reducing them to the comparatively minor ones of being absent without leave from 11 April to 19 May and being in improper possession of Army revolvers. Because of the treatment Cuthbertson and King had received since their return to Britain, they had until then actually had fears that they might be tried on some ridiculous charge such as espionage – or at least with desertion.

They pleaded 'not guilty', maintaining that leaving their unit temporarily was necessary for their scheme, which was patriotic, and that it was essential to 'borrow' pistols for this purpose.

King told the court that he had tried three times to transfer to a fighting unit but was turned down. He had felt he could do something more tangible to help his country. He and Cuthbertson had set out therefore to harass the enemy in any way they could. He said he thought the plan was feasible and that they had gone to France properly armed and equipped. (There must, however, have been some official doubt about his confidence, as better equipment and assistance at both sides of the Channel would have been desired, if not essential, for such a raid.)

Cuthbertson in his evidence told an identical story.

Recalling the two days of the hearing, he says: 'There was little antagonism shown to us by the court, which listened to the story of our adventures with what seemed kindly interest. Regarding the damage we had done in France, we were asked what we thought we had achieved. I said I thought that if we had upset the enemy in any way and made them realise that a landing such as ours could be made, even with a great deal of luck, it must have helped reduce their morale, however slightly.'

At the end of the trial the president of the court told them that he and his fellow officers regretted that it had been necessary for the two to undergo a court martial, and that rather than punish them, they would have preferred to pin medals on their chests. This statement was strikingly similar to earlier ones that had passed between Major Morton and Colonel Clarke in London describing the two as 'a grand chap King and his pal Cuthbertson' and 'these two braves may have landed and got to work'.

The verdicts of 'guilty' were inevitable, though the president told them: 'You will hear in the next few days what punishment we decide to impose, but I do not think you will find it severe.'

The Army hierarchy, like the Civil Service, revealed the workings of the official mind, but there seems little doubt that the two Dental Corps men, once their expedition was over, presented them with a problem. What was to be done with them? Opinion was divided. Should they be treated as heroes and awarded medals, as had been hinted at the trial? It could be argued that this would encourage a spirit of enterprise. On the other hand, others of strictly military mind could – and no doubt did – point out that the two had, after all, deserted, albeit technically, and one just could not have British deserters going off on wild expeditions without permission and indulging themselves in private commando raids. In the event, they were put on trial, though presumably people such as Major Morton and Colonel Clarke had a mitigating influence on the court martial, so that the sentences were not too harsh. It was even believed, though never proved, that Winston Churchill, who had received their letter in the first place, took a personal interest in their case.

News that the court martial had taken place, with a short and guarded version of the adventure, was allowed through by the censor and certain newspapers published it on 10 July, the day after the trial.

A clipping from one of these newspapers was placed on Major Morton's desk at Downing Street with a note from his assistant: 'Have you seen this, please? I think I will draw the War Office's attention to it. F.D.W.B.'

Major Morton replied with the following note:

Mr Brown,

Thank you for letting me see the attached. I suggest that in addition to drawing the attention of the War Office to it, you should make sure that the right Department of the War Office is aware that these men did indeed write to the Prime Minister as they claim. There is no legal value in their having done this, but, as you know, military law is less legalistic than civil law. It is evidence of sincere intention and ought to be brought to the notice of the authority convening the Court.

I am drawing the attention of SOE to the matter.

I think you should ask the War Office to let you know for the Prime Minister what sentence is confirmed upon these men by the convening authority in case some legalistically-minded idiot sentences them to be shot or something.

D.M.

10 July 1942

At the same time the War Office was writing to Major Morton's office, the following letter being despatched:

10 July 1942

Dear Brown,

You will remember your correspondence with Morrison in May about Sergeant King and Private Cuthbertson, who had disappeared from their unit and were thought to have gone off to France by themselves.

As you will no doubt have seen from today's Press, they have since returned to this country and were tried by court martial yesterday. The decision of the court has not yet been promulgated.

Yours sincerely,

S. Redman.

F. D. Brown Esq.

Two days later, on 12 July, Mr Brown replied:

Dear Redman,

Many thanks for your letter of 10 July about Sergeant King and Private Cuthbertson and the expedition to France.

I had, as a matter of fact, been on the point of writing to you, when I saw the story in the Press, to say that I assumed the right department at the War Office and the convening authority of the Court Martial were aware that it was indeed a fact that King had actually written to the Prime Minister as he claimed. It is direct evidence of sincere intention even if nothing more. When the decision of the court is finally promulgated, I should be very glad if you would let me know what the verdict is.

Yours sincerely,
F.D.W.B.

S. Redman Esq.
War Office

It is obvious that those at the War Office and Downing Street who had followed the story almost from the beginning and were keeping a watching brief on the final chapter thought well of the two soldiers who had carried out the daring raid. Their letters revealed a hint of amusement at the behaviour of the amateur saboteurs, none at all of being outraged at their action, and provided the sentence did not turn out to be in their opinion too severe, they were ready to bow discreetly out of the matter.

22 — Question in the House

Sergeant King, as his Army records showed, had no near relatives to be concerned about his wartime activities. Cuthbertson's family, however, had spent some ten anxious weeks unrelieved by any official notification about him.

It was mid-April when that anxiety had been first aroused by the civilian police investigating the possibility of his being at home and informing them then that he had been posted as absent without leave from his unit. Twelve days later they had received the letter he sent in which he informed them that he was going abroad 'on a mission' – a strange assignment for a lad of nineteen who had not been in the Army more than a few months. His parents remained puzzled, but all they could assume was that the two items of news, that from the police and that contained in their son's letter, were connected in some way known only to the Army and whoever had organised 'the mission', whatever it might be. They kept the news in his letter strictly to themselves, believing that whatever their son was doing was of a secret nature and that their silence on the matter was in his interests. Nevertheless, they were understandably worried.

Though he returned to Britain on 19 May, they were unaware of it, their first knowledge of what had happened coming from the report they read in a newspaper on 10 July that he had faced charges at a court martial the previous day.

In the meantime Mrs Cuthbertson had divulged the 'secret' of his mission to one person outside the family, Leslie's fiancée, May Forster, and also confided in her about the visit of the police to the house. May recalled that Leslie told her that, if ever he got into trouble with the Army, he would go to Shaftoe Crags, a Northumberland beauty spot some eighteen miles from where they lived in the Newcastle-upon-Tyne area. It was a place they had often visited together during their courtship. Mrs Cuthbertson and May made two abortive visits to the spot.

Another attempt they made to unravel the mystery, one on less orthodox lines, had a somewhat interesting result: they visited a fortune-teller at Walker-upon-Tyne, telling her that Leslie was missing from his Army unit, though they told her nothing about his letter and what it contained. They handed her a photograph showing the members of his unit. Both King, of whom they knew nothing, and Leslie were shown on it, but not near to each other. The fortune-teller pointed to King and informed Mrs Cuthbertson that he was with her son and that, whatever they were doing, all would be well in the end with both soldiers.

The erstwhile adventurers were no longer confined to cells or kept incommunicado in any way, and nine days after the court martial, on 18 July they were called before their own CO to be informed of the sentences the court had decided to impose.

Sergeant King was reduced in rank to corporal and immediately went free. For him the punishment was particularly light, especially when studied in the context of a statement given to the court martial by his defending officer that he would willingly have given up all his stripes to be posted to a combatant unit.

Private Cuthbertson, however, had no stripes to lose and was sentenced to twenty-eight days' detention, a far greater penalty by comparison when taking into consideration that a stay in a detention-centre for servicemen entailed far more than confinement and was generally looked upon with horror by any soldier unfortunate enough to be sent to such a prison, known colloquially as 'the glasshouse'.

The sentences provide an interesting commentary on the vagaries of life that the sergeant, who technically at least should have held the greater responsibility for the 'crime', suffered far less than the unfortunate and much younger soldier

The court martial also ordered that no record of the 'crime' should appear on any Army document or on any of their personal papers.

Outside the CO's office the two had the opportunity of a brief word together. King assured his comrade that he would be seeing him again when his imprisonment was over. But, as it happened, it was the last time they ever met or received any communication from each other.

Though there was afterwards less chance of their meeting, King being posted to another unit before Cuthbertson returned from his prison sentence and he himself being sent later to an infantry regiment, it remains perhaps a little strange that they were never again in contact after sharing such a remarkable adventure. For many years Cuthbertson believed that the Army, which certainly before the court martial had regarded them as dangerous men, felt that it might be preferable for them to be kept apart for the remaining years of the war.

On 19 July, the day after the sentences were promulgated, the Cuthbertsons' local vicar at Newcastle made mention of the matter in his sermon. He said: 'Thomas Cuthbertson was a sergeant in our Boys' Brigade company. While we cannot but admire his courage, at the same time we cannot but question the wisdom of his exploit.'

Cuthbertson's father was far from satisfied with the result of the court martial. He sent a telegram to the Secretary of State for War, Sir James Grigg, asking him to cancel his son's prison sentence and emphasising that his son had already been under arrest for more than two months and that his action in carrying out the commando raid with King was prompted by a desire to serve his country.

In addition, Mr Ivor Thomas, the MP for Keighley, asked the Secretary for War, in the House of Commons on 28 July, whether, in order to encourage an offensive spirit throughout the Army, he would remit the sentences on Sergeant King and Private Cuthbertson, of the Army Dental Corps, who had recently taken a motor-boat to France without authority, or alternatively reduce the sentences to reprimand.

Sir James Grigg replied that the sentences had been confirmed by the appropriate military authorities, and he was not prepared to override their judgment. But he added:

'I quite appreciate the desire of these men for a more combative life and will make arrangements for them to be transferred to an arm where I hope it can be gratified.'

The War Office duly informed 10 Downing Street of the sentences. The letter read:

5 August 1942

Dear Brown,

You will no doubt have seen the answer the Secretary of State gave in the House on 29 July about the famous case of Sergeant King and Private Cuthbertson of the Army Dental Corps.

You may like to know that Sergeant King has now been posted to the Commando Depot, and Private Cuthbertson has been transferred to the Durham Light Infantry.

Yours sincerely,
N. G. Morrison.

F. D. W. Brown Esq.

Mr Brown pencilled a note on the letter before passing it to Major Morton: 'I think this a rather good end to this story. They are not being executed and are getting what they want – after, I imagine, a little detention! F.D.W.B.'

And that, so far as all were concerned, even those who had championed the two, was that. All, that is, except for poor Leslie Cuthbertson, whose detention at Fort Darland, Chatham, still had a week to go.

What was somewhat lightly dismissed as 'a little detention', was, by the very nature of Army prison treatment, a very unpleasant experience. Mr Cuthbertson recalls: 'Everything we did, everywhere we moved, was at the double. Some sergeants carried sticks and lashed out at anyone who didn't move fast enough. Sometimes we had to wear gasmasks and were either sick in them because we couldn't get our breath or fell down exhausted. Then the sergeants gathered round and kicked you till you got to your feet. I was kicked over and over again. Some appeared to be sadists, like Belsen guards.'

In contrast to the sentence he served, he received letters from total strangers, congratulating him on 'showing the right spirit' and offering him free holidays. His father in Newcastle-upon-Tyne received letters from many parts of

Britain expressing sympathy with him because his son had been court-martialled. One was from an Army officer commiserating with Mr Cuthbertson but, like some others before him, noting that the sentence 'had not been severe'.

It has nevertheless been said that an experience of any duration in an Armed Services' 'glasshouse' tended to leave a permanent scar on anyone unfortunate enough to be imprisoned in one. It could not have failed to embitter for quite a long period a lad of nineteen who believed his act to have been highly patriotic and whose companion in the venture had merely lost one of the stripes on his arm. It is certain that it was the means of changing his attitude towards the Army – an attitude that could not in the first place have been more enthusiastic and praiseworthy, despite the illegality of the escapade. This is no doubt illustrated in the fact that he afterwards turned down a suggestion made by his CO that he be recommended to be sent to an Officer Cadet Training Unit with a view to being commissioned in a combatant unit. This offer was made when, after gaining four days' remission for good conduct, he was posted straight to the Durham Light Infantry.

The disillusioning effect of his detention did not, however, prevent his having a successful Army career: he became an instructor at the Army School of Physical Training and gained the highest of the non-commissioned ranks – that of warrant-officer.

Nor did it prevent his making a great success of his civilian life after the war. He married his fiancée, May Forster, whose concern had led her to seek comfort from a fortune-teller and who became a social worker in Newcastle's tough Scotswood Road area.

The spirit of enterprise that had already characterised the escapade to France was again displayed by his building up several successful companies and becoming a prominent member of Newcastle-upon-Tyne City Council, in 1967 being Deputy Lord Mayor. He now owns and runs his own plant-hire company, a garage and petrol-station and a motor-car sales business.

Peter King also continued to demonstrate the qualities that had led to their own private little war. He was commissioned in the Commandos, served in the Lovat Scouts, gained an MC and ended the war as a lieutenant. But that was not the end of his military service: after the war he went to New Zealand and was in that country's contingent which served in the Korean War.

Lieutenant-Colonel J. W. Moodie, DSO, of Dunedin, New Zealand, gave this account of Peter King's Korean service:

> I first met him in 1950 when volunteers were called to form the 16th Field Artillery Regiment to go to Korea as New Zealand's contribution to the United Nations. I was given the job of forming this regiment and subsequently commanding it in Korea.
>
> Lieutenant Peter King, MC, was one of the first volunteers, and after going through a conversion course from infantry to artillery, he was given command of a troop of guns and promoted to captain.
>
> In this capacity he served with distinction, and on one memorable occasion he very nearly earned a VC. As it was, he was given the immediate award of a DSO, which means that he just missed the coveted award.
>
> He was manning his observation-post in a forward platoon area of the Kings' Own Scottish Borderers when the Chinese attacked in force. Almost immediately the observation-post's radio was knocked out, the telephone lines cut and Captain King wounded. The infantry sustained heavy casualties and some of them withdrew. Captain King rallied the remnants of the platoon, made several trips under fire to Company HQ for more grenades and, with his little band, held the hill most of that day.
>
> During this effort he was wounded several times and was engaged in numerous hand-to-hand conflicts with the attacking waves of Chinese – repelling all of them. His last wound was in the leg, and eventually he had to be carried out to safety and evacuation to hospital.
>
> Two months later he was back in the regiment as a battery commander promoted to major and was still there when I relinquished my command in April 1952.
>
> I next saw him at the royal investiture held in Christchurch during Her Majesty's visit to New Zealand in 1953 when Peter was invested with his DSO.

After the Korean war, Peter King took a job with the New Zealand forestry service. He was killed in 1962 when his Land-Rover overturned on a sharp bend.

Author's Note

My thanks for assistance during research are due in particular and in great measure to Mr T. L. Cuthbertson, one of the two men who took part in the operation – and to that gratitude I should like to add my own admiration for the spirit shown by him and his comrade in the action.

A SELECTION OF NON-FICTION TITLES ON THE SPHERE LIST . . .

WAR NON-FICTION			
DORA	Jean Michel	£1.75	☐
McINDOE'S ARMY	Peter Williams & Ted Harrison	£1.50	☐
AGAINST ALL ODDS	R. Foxall	£1.50	☐
EAGLE DAY	Richard Collier	£4.75	☐
PLAYING FOR TIME	Fania Fenelon	£1.25	☐
THE THIRD WORLD WAR	General Sir John Hackett	£2.25	☐
A MAN CALLED INTREPID	William Stevenson	£1.95	☐
BIOGRAPHY & AUTOBIOGRAPHY			
MARY	Patricia Collins	£1.50	☐
MAJESTY	Robert Lacey	£1.50	☐
PHILBY: THE SPY WHO BETRAYED A GENERATION	B. Page, D. Leitch & P. Knightly	£1.25	☐
A WAY TO DIE	Rosemary & Victor Zorza	£1.50	☐
MY STORY	Ingrid Bergman	£1.95	☐
EMMA V.I.P.	Sheila Hocken	£1.25	☐
TRUE BRITT	Britt Ekland	£1.50	☐
WILL	G. Gordon Liddy	£1.75	☐
THE SPECIAL YEARS	Val Doonican	£1.25	☐
REFERENCE			
REPAIRING HOUSES	Trevor James	£5.95	☐
ROGET'S THESAURUS	Edited by D. C. Browning	£2.10	☐
THE GALLUP REPORT	Norman Webb & Robert Wybrow	£1.95	☐

All Sphere books are available at your local bookshop or newsagent, or can be ordered direct from the publisher. Just tick the titles you want and fill in the form below.

Name ______________________________

Address ______________________________

____

Write to Sphere Books, Cash Sales Department, P.O. Box 11, Falmouth, Cornwall TR10 9EN

Please enclose a cheque or postal order to the value of the cover price plus:

UK: 40p for the first book, 18p for the second book and 13p for each additional book ordered to a maximum charge of £1.49.

OVERSEAS: 60p for the first book plus 18p per copy for each additional book.

BFPO & EIRE: 40p for the first book, 18p for the second book plus 13p per copy for the next 7 books, thereafter 7p per book.

Sphere Books reserve the right to show new retail prices on covers which may differ from those previously advertised in the text or elsewhere, and to increase postal rates in accordance with the PO.